Essential Music Theory © 2022 by San Marco Publications. All rights reserved.

All right reserved. No part of this book may be reproduced in any form or by electronic or mechanical means including Information storage and retrieval systems without permission in writing from the author.

ISNB: 9781896499317

Contents

Lesson 1: **Accidentals**	1
Lesson 2: **Time**	5
Lesson 3: **Major Scales**	18
Lesson 4: **History 1**	26
Review 1	30
Lesson 5: **Minor Scales**	33
Lesson 6: **Intervals**	40
Lesson 7: **Chords**	50
Lesson 8: **History 2**	64
Review 2	67
Lesson 9: **Cadences**	70
Lesson 10: **Transposition**	76
Lesson 11: **Melody**	82
Lesson 12: **History 3**	90
Review 3	93
Lesson 13: **Music Analysis**	96
Music Terms and Signs	103
Exam	109

1
Accidentals

Notes are altered by the use of signs called *accidentals*. Accidentals raise or lower the pitch of a note.

    Sharp   ♯   Double-sharp   𝄪

    Flat   ♭   Double-flat   ♭♭

    Natural   ♮

The Double Sharp

A ***double-sharp*** raises a note by a whole step or two half steps and looks like this: x . Double sharps are not very common but are sometimes required to spell a chord or interval correctly.

Figure 1.1

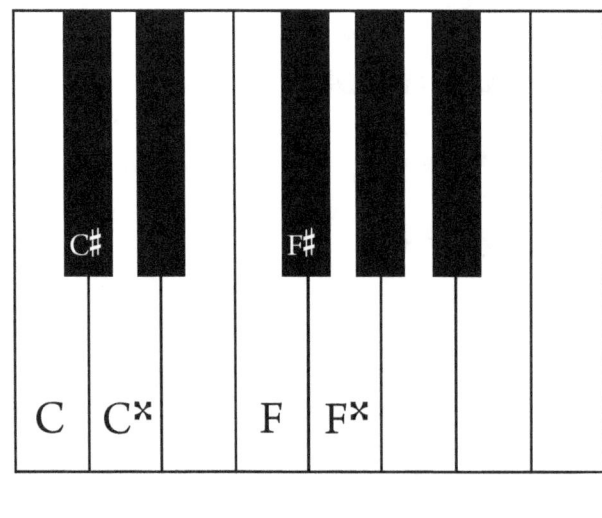

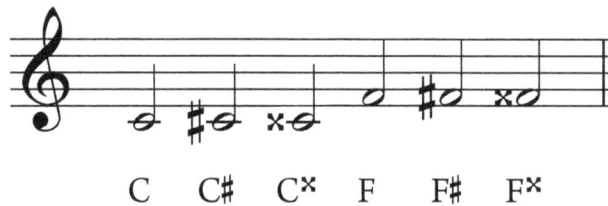

©San Marco Publications 2022   1   Accidentals

1. Apply double-sharps to each note

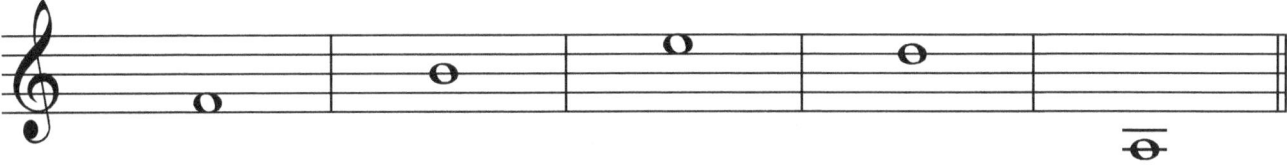

The Double Flat

A *double-flat* lowers a note by a whole step or two half steps and looks like this: ♭♭. Like double-sharps, double-flats occur rarely.

Figure 1.2

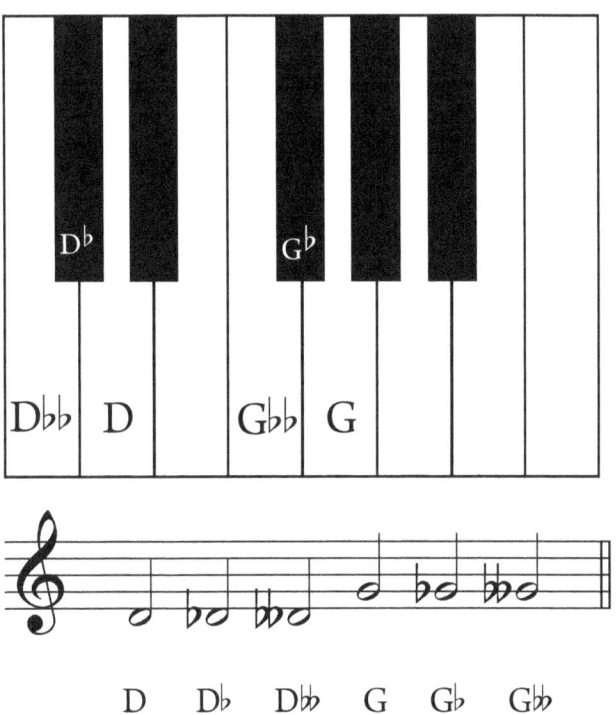

2. Apply double-flats to each note

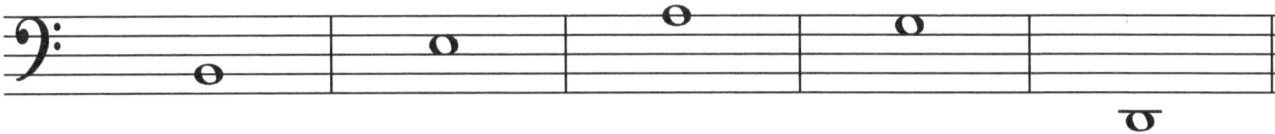

Enharmonic Equivalents

With the use of double-sharps and double-flats, every note except G♯/A♭ can have three names.

Figure 1.3 illustrates that the note G can be G, F𝄪, or A♭♭. These notes are considered *enharmonic equivalents*. This means that they are the same pitch but have different names, like F♯ and G♭.

Figure 1.3

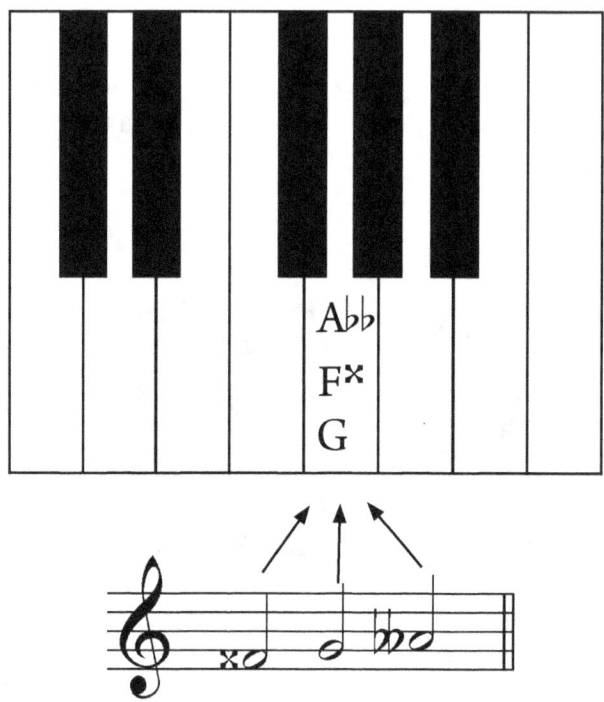

1. Write two enharmonic equivalents for each of the following notes.

2. Rewrite the following melodies in the other clef without changing the pitch.

2
Time

The Thirty-Second Note and Rest

A single thirty-second note is written with three flags (Figure 2.1). Thirty-second notes are grouped using three beams to join the notes (Figure 2.2). The thirty-second rest uses three hooks placed in the top three spaces of the staff (Figure 2.3). The thirty-second note is half the duration of a sixteenth note.

Figure 2.1

Figure 2.2

Figure 2.3

Figure 2.4

A thirty-second note triplet is equal to one sixteenth note.

Figure 2.5

1. Name one note which lasts as long as the number of thirty second notes in each of the following.

   a. 2 thirty-second notes last as long as a _____ note.

   b. 4 thirty-second notes last as long as an _____ note.

   c. 16 thirty-second notes last as long as a _____ note.

   d. 12 thirty-second notes last as long as a _____ note.

   e. 32 thirty-second notes last as long as a _____ note.

   f. 8 thirty-second notes last as long as a _____ note.

2. Write the correct time signature for the following.

A dot placed next to a sixteenth note increases its value by half. A dotted sixteenth note is usually connected to a thirty-second note as seen on beats 1 and 3 in Figure 2.6.

Figure 2.6

1. Add the missing rest or rests under each bracket.

2. Add the bar lines to the following according to the time signatures.

Compound Time

A time signature that is in simple time has 2, 3, or 4 for the top number. A compound time signature has 6, 9, or 12 for the top number. Simple and compound time can be duple, triple or quadruple, depending on the number of beats in each measure.

Compound time breaks itself into groups of three. Compound duple time equals two groups of three, and the top number is 6. Compound triple equals three groups of three, and the top number is 9. Compound quadruple equals four groups of three, and the top number is 12. The main beat is a dotted note, since a dotted note can be divided into three equal parts. Let's examine the three types of compound time.

Compound Duple Time

Compound duple time has two beats in each measure. Each beat is equal to three pulses. In compound duple time, the upper number of the time signature is always 6. The lower number may be 8, 4, or 16.

Figure 2.7 shows three different compound duple time signatures. The first measure, in 6/8 time, contains six eighth note pulses. The main beat is a dotted quarter since it represents one group of three pulses.

In 6/4 time, there are six quarter note pulses in each measure. The main beat is a dotted half note since it represents one group of three quarter note pulses.

Figure 2.7

1. Add bar lines according to the time signatures. Circle each beat (group of 3 pulses).

Compound Triple Time

Compound triple time has 3 beats (3 groups of 3) in each measure. In 9/8 time there are 9 eighth notes in every measure. These are 9 pulses. There are 3 groups of 3 pulses which are considered 3 beats. Each beat is equal to a dotted note. In compound triple time the upper number of the time signature is always 9. The lower number may be 8, 4, or 16.

Figure 2.8

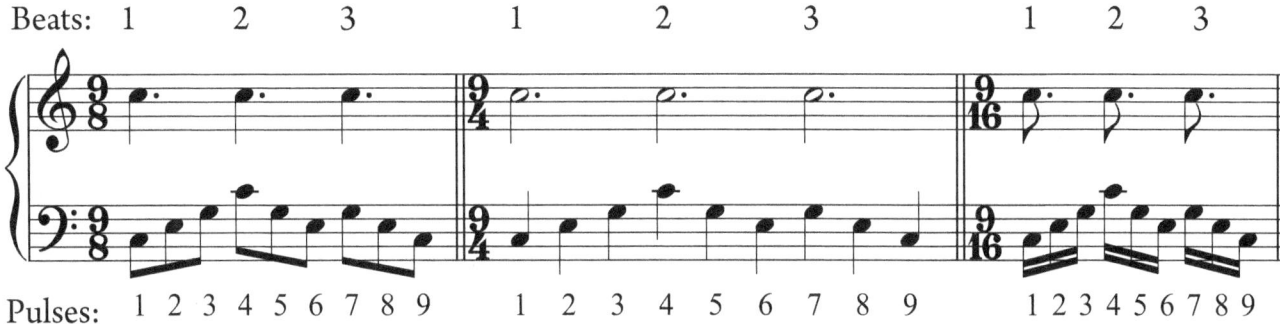

2. Add time signatures at the beginning of each line. Circle each beat (group of 3 pulses).

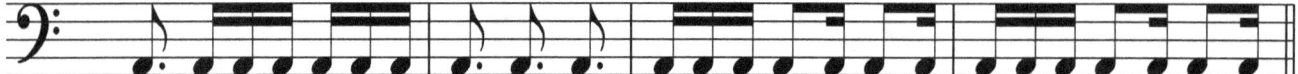

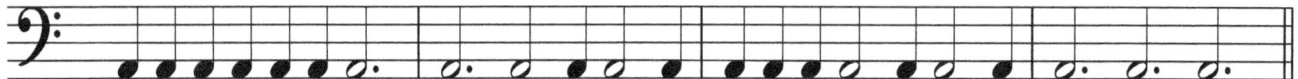

Compound Quadruple Time

Compound quadruple time has 4 beats (4 groups of 3) in each measure. In 12/8 time there are 12 eighth notes in every measure. We consider this 12 pulses. There are 4 groups of 3 pulses which are considered 4 beats. Each beat is equal to a dotted note. In compound quadruple time the upper number of the time signature is always 12. The lower number may be 8, 4, or 16.

Figure 2.9

3. Add bar lines according to the time signatures. Circle each beat (group of 3 pulses).

Grouping Notes in Compound Time

In compound time notes and rests are grouped to show each beat as clearly as possible.

Figure 2.10 contains two measures of 9/8 time. In this time signature, the main beat is equal to a dotted quarter note. The notes in each measure are organized to reflect this. All notes belonging to one beat are placed together.

Figure 2.10

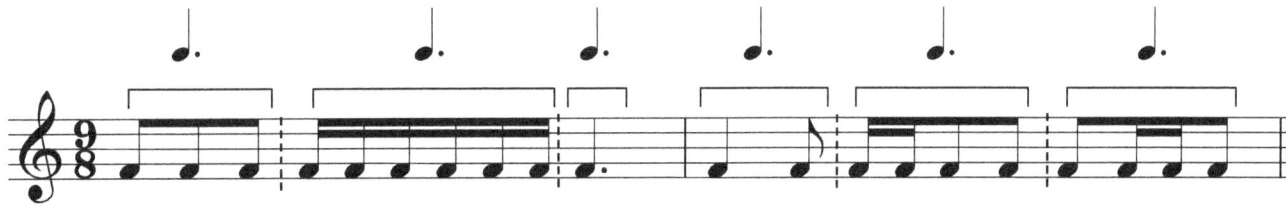

Figure 2.11 illustrates the difference in note grouping between 6/8 and 3/4 time. 6/8 is compound *duple* time, and the notes are placed into two groups of three. 3/4 is simple *triple* time, and the notes are organized into three groups of two.

Figure 2.11

4. Rewrite the following passages grouping them according to the time signature.

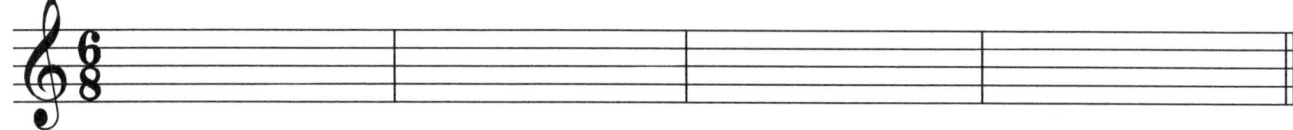

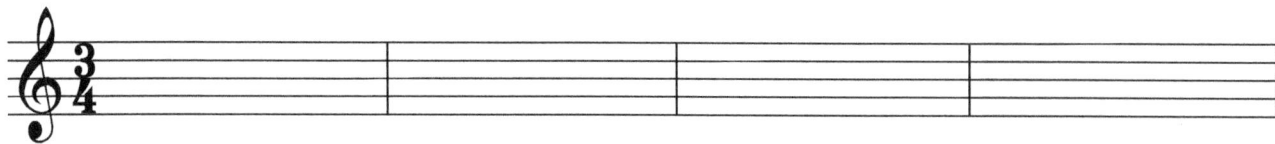

Rests in Compound Time

Dotted rests are not used in simple time. These rests are only used in compound time and represent one beat. Two beats may be joined into one dotted rest to represent the first half or the last half of a measure of compound quadruple time.

Figure 2.12

In compound time, each beat equals 3 pulses. The first 2 pulses of a beat should be joined into one rest as shown in Figure 2.13 a) and b). The last 2 pulses of a beat should use separate rests as shown in Figure 2.13 c) and d). Never join pulse 2 with pulse 3.

Figure 2.13

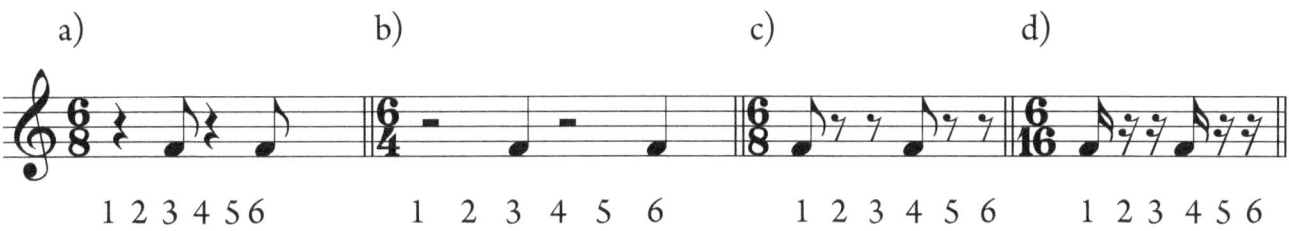

In compound triple time beats 1 and 2 may be joined into one rest. Do not join beats 2 and 3 into one rest.

Figure 2.14

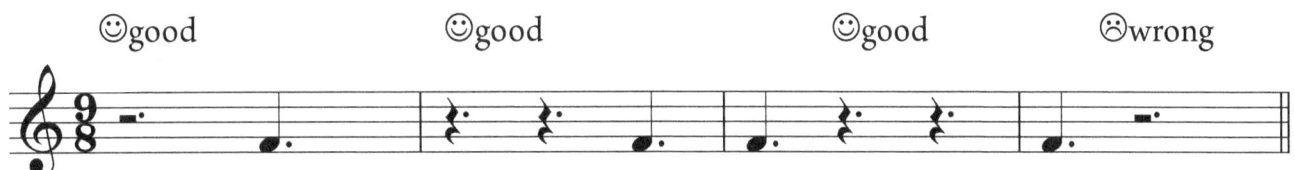

In compound quadruple time beats 1 and 2 should be joined into one rest. Beats 3 and 4 should be joined into one rest. Do not join beats 2 and 3 into one rest.

Figure 2.15

5. Add rests under the brackets to complete each measure.

6. Add the correct time signature to the following.

Girolamo Frescobaldi
La Spagnoletta

Cesar Franck
Symphonic Variations

Joseph Haydn
Symphony in B flat, IV

Muzio Clementi
Sonata for 4 hands

Ludwig van Beethoven
Sonata Op. 31, No. 1

Albert Roussel,
Le Festin de L'Araignee

3
Major Scales

Circle of Fifths

Figure 3.1

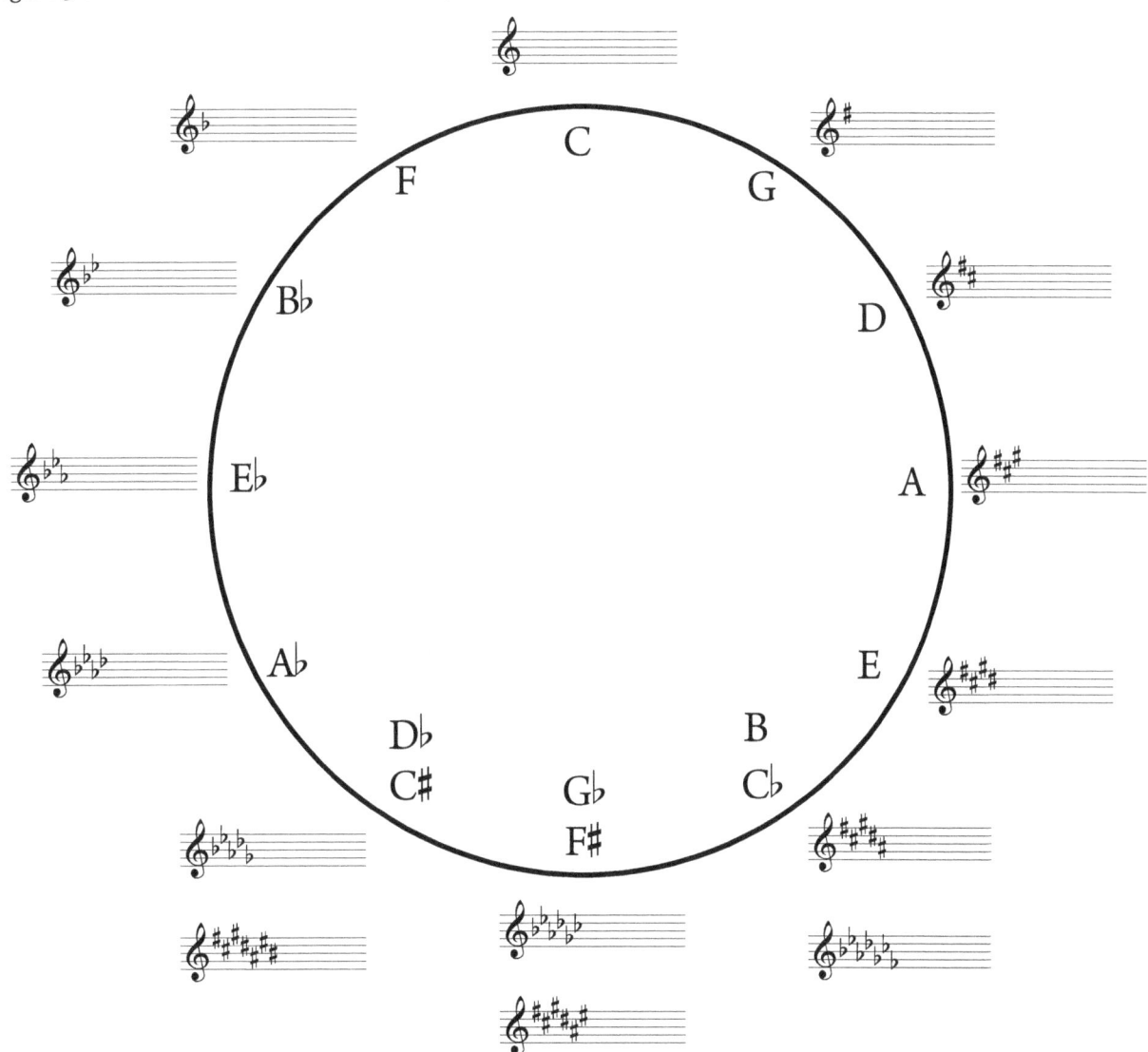

The *circle of 5ths* (Figure 3.1), is a chart organizing all of the keys into a system that can be used to relate them to one another. At the top, is the key of C major, which has no sharps or flats in its key signature. Each stop on the circle moving clockwise from C is a key with one more sharp than the previous key. Each stop moving counter-clockwise from C is a key with one more flat than the previous key. Each note is a perfect fifth away from another.

Sharp Keys

C major has no sharps or flats.

Figure 3.2 is a list of the sharp keys and where they are located on the staff.
The order of sharps is **F C G D A E B**.

Here is a saying to help you remember the order of sharps:

Fat **C**ats **G**o **D**own **A**lleys **E**ating **B**irds.

Figure 3.2

G

D

A

E

B

F♯

C♯

Major Scales

Flat Keys

Flats within a key signature always follow a specific order.

Figure 3.3 is a list of the flat keys and where they are located on the staff. The order of flats is **B E A D G C F**.

Here is a saying to help you remember the order of flats:

Big **E**lephants **A**lways **D**rive **G**olf **C**arts **F**ast

figure 3.3

1. Name the following major keys and name the sharp and flats in each key.

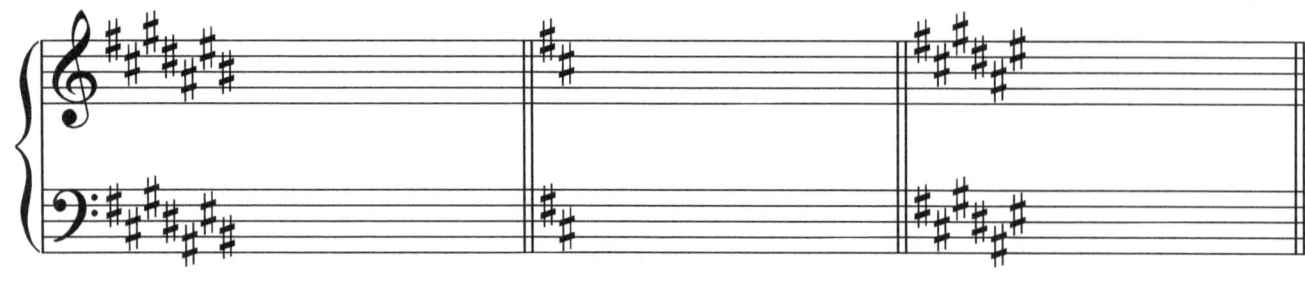

Key: _____   _____   _____

Sharps: _____   _____   _____

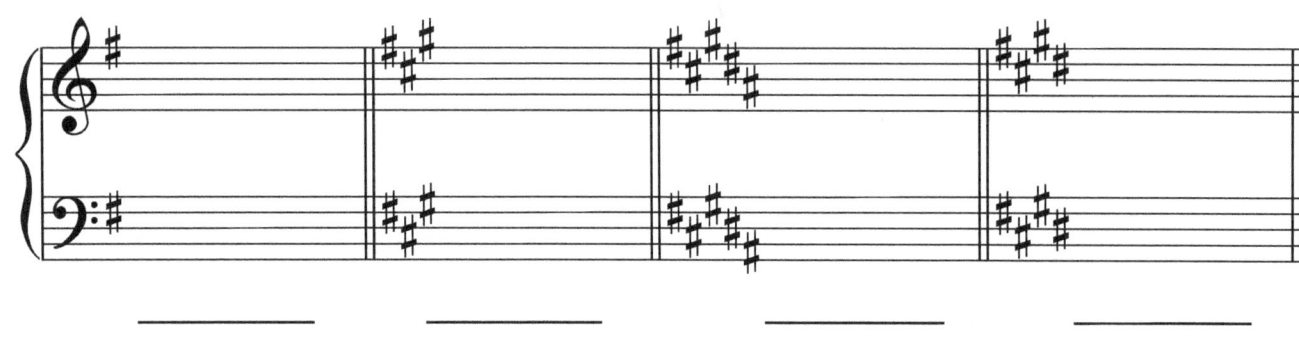

_____   _____   _____   _____

_____   _____   _____   _____

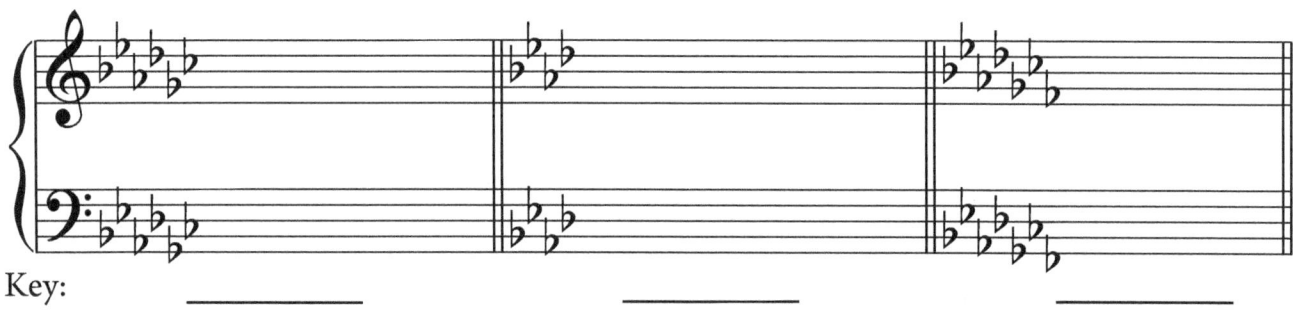

Key: _____   _____   _____

Flats: _____   _____   _____

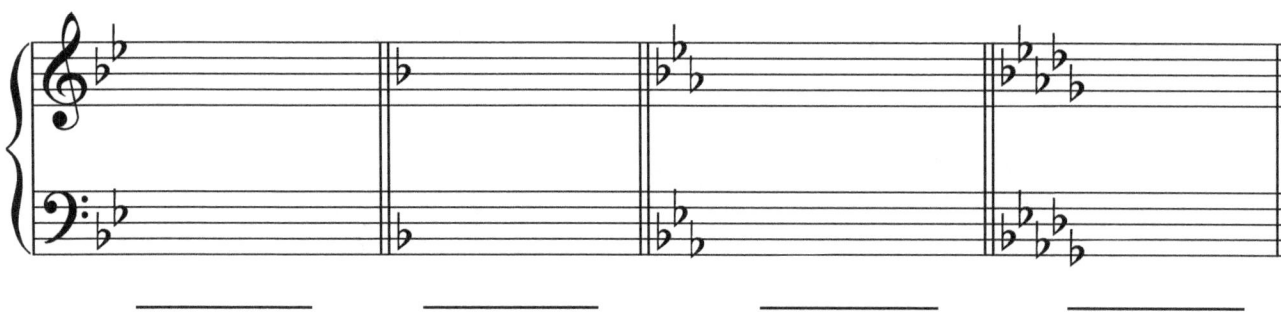

_____   _____   _____   _____

_____   _____   _____   _____

Major Scales

Technical Names for Scale Degrees.

Every scale degree has a technical name. These are the names for each scale degree.

$\hat{1}$ Tonic
$\hat{2}$ Supertonic
$\hat{3}$ Mediant
$\hat{4}$ Subdominant
$\hat{5}$ Dominant
$\hat{6}$ Submediant
$\hat{7}$ Leading tone

1. Write the following major key signatures and notes on the grand staves.

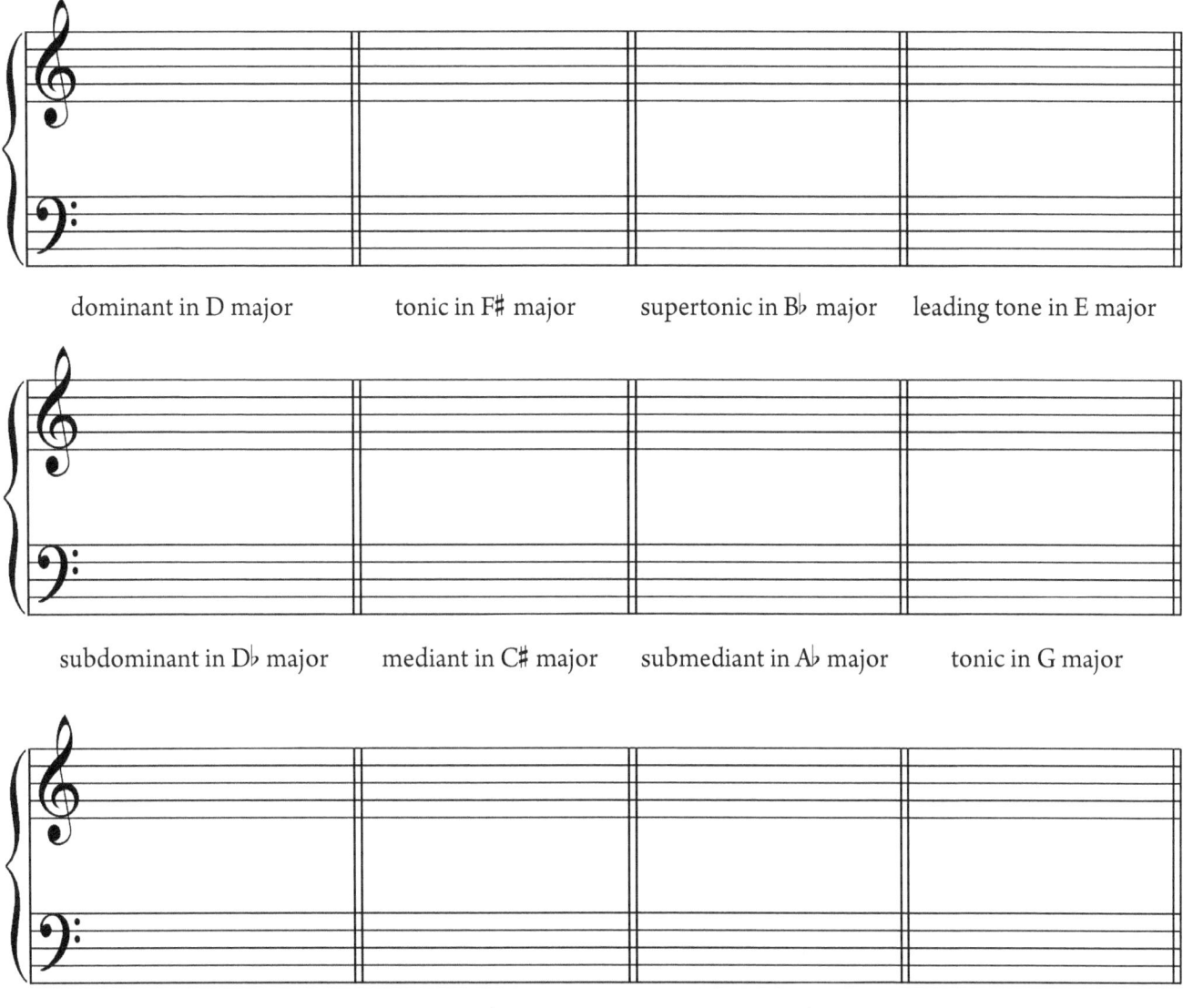

dominant in D major   tonic in F# major   supertonic in B♭ major   leading tone in E major

subdominant in D♭ major   mediant in C# major   submediant in A♭ major   tonic in G major

leading tone in B major   tonic in G♭ major   supertonic in E♭ major   dominant in A major

2. Write the following scales ascending and descending in wholes notes using a key signature for each.

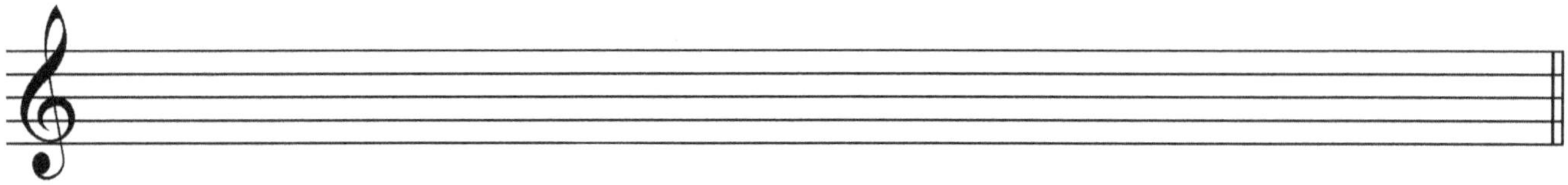

E major

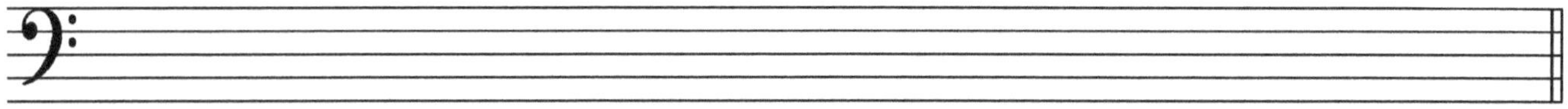

A♭ major

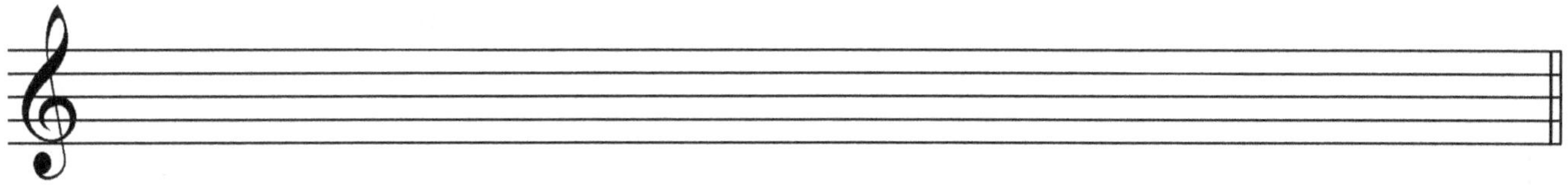

D♭ major

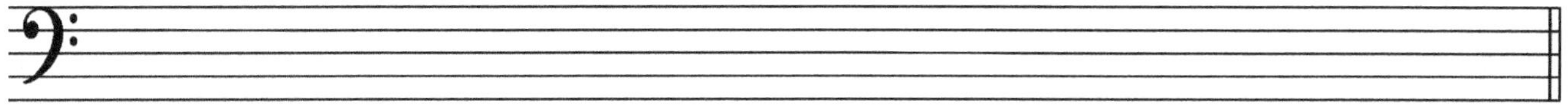

G major

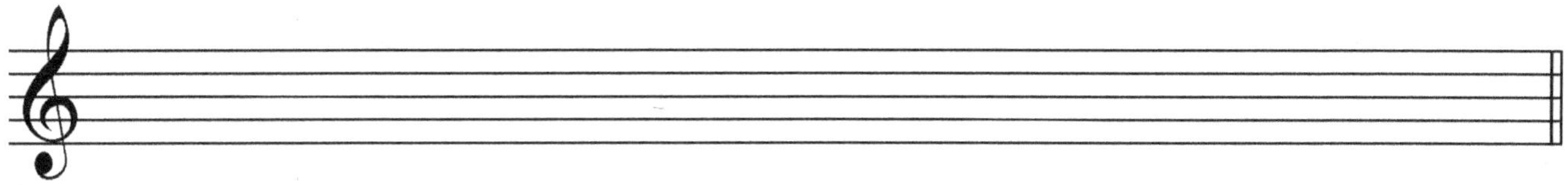

B major

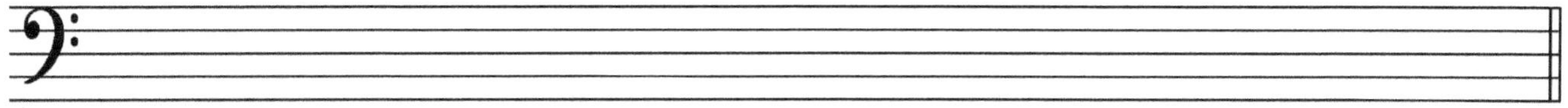

F major

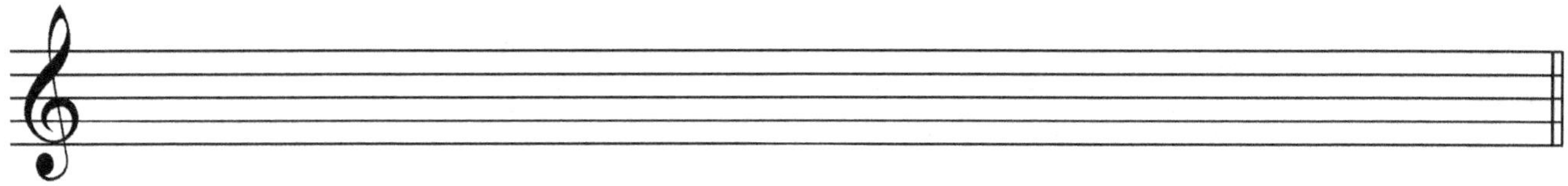

D major

Major Scales

3. Add clefs and accidentals to create the following major scales.

Eb major

A major

F# major

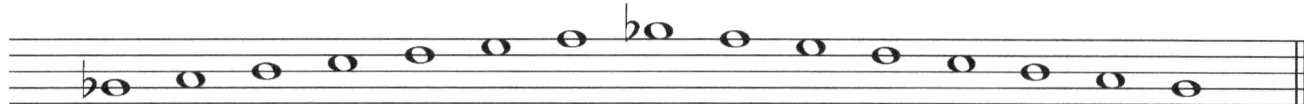

Bb major

C# major

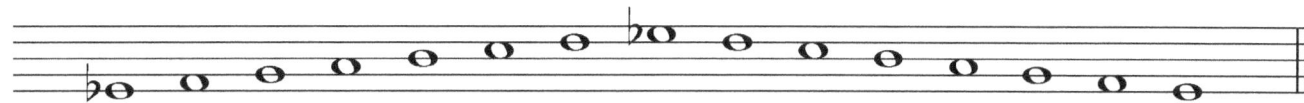

Gb major

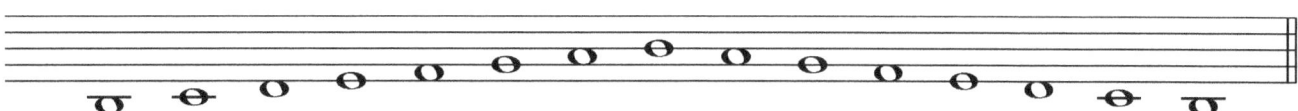

B major

4. Write the following scales ascending and descending using half notes.

The major scale with 5 flats

The major scale with D as the leading tone

The major scale with C# as the supertonic

The major scale with D# as the submediant

The major scale with one flat

The major scale with A as the subdominant

The major scale with F as the dominant

©San Marco Publications 2022

Major Scales

4
History 1

The Baroque Era (ca 1600 - 1750)

The word ***Baroque*** is used to describe a style of art from a specific period in history. *Art* can mean a lot of things. Here, it applies to painting, architecture, and most importantly to our field of study, music.

All Baroque art, architecture, and music was created around 1600 to 1750. However, Baroque music is a style of music. It is not an exact period of time.

What is the Baroque style?

Artists of the Baroque period attempted to evoke emotions in the listener by appealing to their senses. A composer could create a piece of music that would make the listener feel a specific emotion (sadness, happiness, etc.). This was known as ***the doctrine of the affections***.

Baroque music is tuneful, very organized, and its melodies are often highly decorated and elaborate. This music can be quite dramatic.

A lot of Baroque music is ***contrapuntal*** or based on ***counterpoint***. This means that there can be many different lines of music (or melodies) all going their own way. These single melodies weave together to make a whole piece of music.

The best way to understand Baroque music, is to listen to the great Baroque composers.

There are many great composers from the Baroque era. The greatest one is Johann Sebastian Bach (1685–1750).

Other famous baroque composers include:

Johann Pachelbel (1653–1706)
Antonio Vivaldi (1678–1741)
George Frideric Handel (1685–1759)

Johann Sebastian Bach (1685 - 1750)

Johann Sebastian Bach was born in Eisenach, Germany, where his father, a musician, taught him to play violin and harpsichord. By the time Johann was 10, both his parents had died. Johann was raised by his older brother who was a church organist. Johann also became a very skilled organist.

Bach's life has three major periods.

The Weimar period. Bach worked for the Duke of Weimar. In this period he became an organ virtuoso and wrote many great works for the instrument.

The Cöthen period. Bach worked for the Prince of Anhalt-Cöthen. During this period he composed a lot of chamber music including suites, instrumental sonatas, and the Brandenburg Concertos.

The Leipzig period. During this period Bach became the cantor, organist, and music composer for St. Thomas Lutheran Church in Leipzig, Germany. Bach remained there for the rest of his life.

Bach wrote music for keyboard instruments (harpsichord, clavichord, organ), orchestra, choirs, chamber groups, and many solo instruments. He is considered one of the greatest musical geniuses in history. In fact, he is such an important composer, that the year of his death (1750), is used to mark the end of the Baroque Era.

Two-part Invention in C major, BWV 772 - J.S. Bach

Bachs *Inventions and Sinfonias,* also known as the *Two and Three-Part Inventions* are a collection of thirty pieces for keyboard. There are 15 two-part and 15 three-part inventions in the masterpiece. Bach said that he composed the Inventions "for amateurs of the keyboard to achieve a cantabile style of playing in two and three parts." They were written as musical teaching pieces for his students.
The two-part inventions were composed in the Cöthen period, and the three-part inventions (Sinfonias)were completed at the beginning of the Leipzig period.

Polyphony is the performance of multiple melodies at the same time. It's a little like two people giving speeches next to each other, but the speeches are different. Imagine having four speakers giving four different speeches at the same time. Eventually, rules developed to control these multiple melodies. These rules became known as ***counterpoint*** or the practice of controlling the relationship between the different melodies.

Polyphony is one of the musical textures. ***Texture*** is how you hear the music. It may sound dense, thick, thin, or a number of different ways. Polyphony is typically described as thick or densely textured, due to the independence of multiple melodic lines.

An invention is a short composition for a keyboard instrument using two-part ***counterpoint***. In a two-part invention, there are two lines of music that interweave with one another. As a result, two part inventions are ***polyphonic***.

Inventions use techniques we have covered in past melody writing lessons. These are:

- ***motives***: short melodic and rhythmic ideas used to create a melody
- ***imitation***: the technique of repeating a musical idea (motive) in another voice or part.
- ***sequence***: the repetition of a motive or phrase at a higher or lower pitch.

Figure 4.1 contains the opening four measures of J.S. Bach's Two-Part Invention in C major, BWV 772. BWV is a numbering system used to identify Bach's compositions. This invention is based on a seven note motive found in m.1. Imitation of the opening motive can be found in the bass clef in m.1. A sequence moving downward can be found in mm.3 and 4.

Figure 4.1

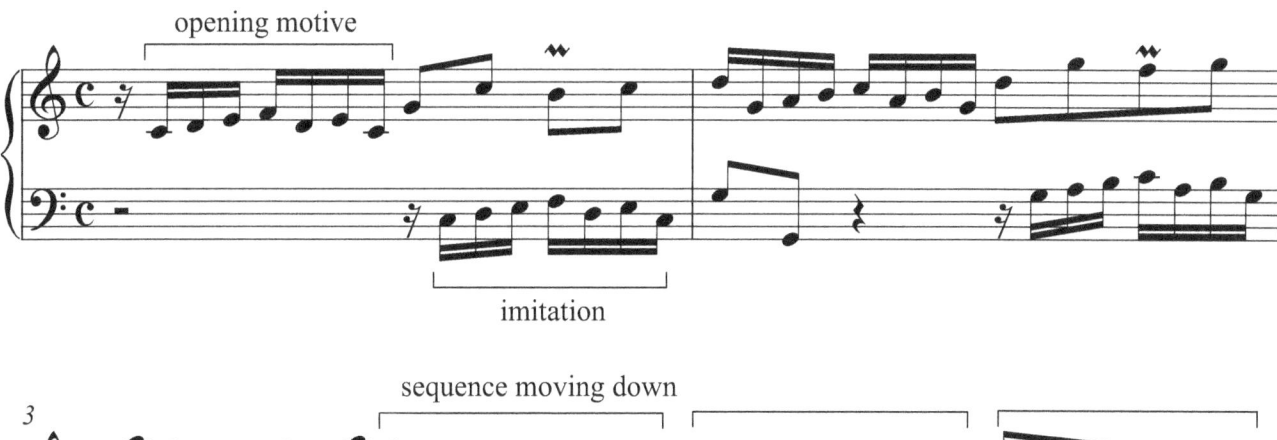

Music Terms

Study the following music terms

ben, bene	well
col, coll', colla, colle	with
con	with
con brio	with vigor, spirit
con espressione	with expression
con fuoco	with fire
con grazia	with grace
con moto	with motion
e, ed	and
fortepiano, fp	loud then suddenly soft
grave	slow and solemn

Review 1

1. Give two enharmonic equivalents for the following notes.

   D _____

   F _____

   F♯ _____

   C _____

   B♭ _____

2. Add rests below the brackets to complete each measure.

3. Write the following scales ascending and descending in quarter notes using the correct key signature for each.

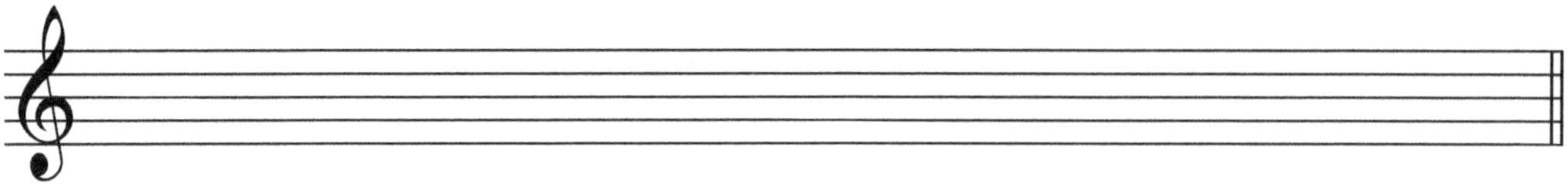

C♯ major

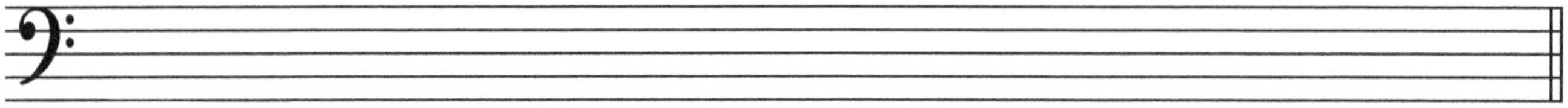

The major scale with A♭ as its dominant

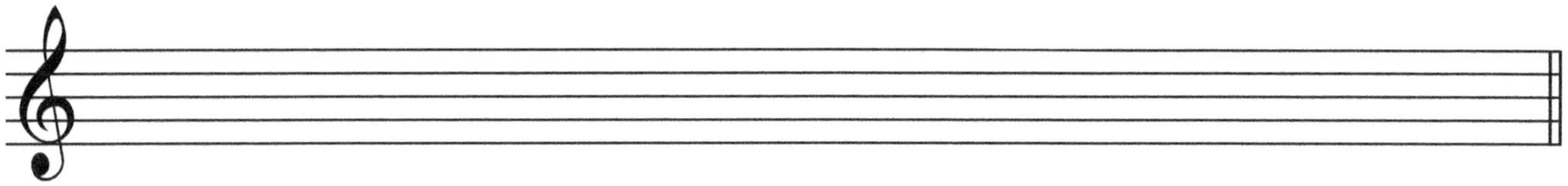

The major scale with 5 sharps

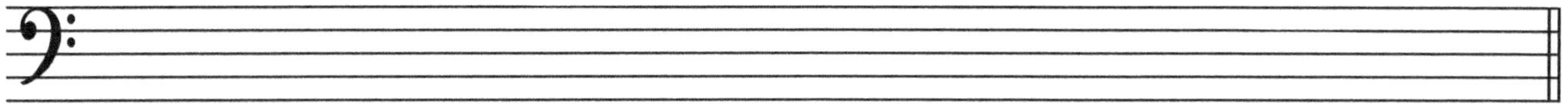

The major scale with E♭ as its submediant

4. Match the following terms with their meanings.

a. *con moto*	____well
b. *con grazia*	____with
c. *con espressione*	____and
d. *grave*	____loud then suddenly soft
e. *fortepiano, fp*	____slow and solemn
f. *con fuoco*	____with fire
g. *con brio*	____with vigor, spirit
h. *e, ed*	____with expression
i. *con*	____with grace
j. *ben, bene*	____with motion

5. Choose the correct answers.

a. The Baroque period occurred approximately:	☐ 1600-1700 ☐ 2010-2015	☐ 1650-1725 ☐ 1600-1750
b. The following are famous Baroque composers:	☐ J.S. Bach ☐ Mozart	☐ Vivaldi ☐ Handel
c. These elements can be used to describe Baroque music:	☐ counterpoint ☐ romantic	☐ doctrine of affections ☐ highly ornamented
d. These are Bach's 3 main periods.	☐ Leipzig ☐ Berlin	☐ Weimar ☐ Cöthen
e. Bach composed for the following mediums.	☐ keyboard ☐ choir	☐ orchestra ☐ chamber music
f. How many 2 part inventions did J.S. Bach write?	☐ 21 ☐ 12	☐ 15 ☐ 6
g. The 3-part inventions are also known as:	☐ sonatas ☐ dances	☐ sinfonias ☐ fugues
h. The 2-part inventions are written for this many voices:	☐ 2 ☐ 6	☐ 3 ☐ 32
i. 3 elements found in the 2-part inventions are:	☐ motives ☐ imitation	☐ sequence ☐ monophony
j. This is the numbering system used to identify Bach's works:	☐ NRA ☐ BVW	☐ BWV ☐ BMW

5
Minor Scales

Relative Keys

Every major key has a *relative minor*. They share the same key signature and are called *relative keys*. The relationship between these relative keys is shown in Figure 5.1. The tonic of the relative minor is located on scale degree $\hat{6}$ of the major scale. Scale degree $\hat{6}$ in C major is A. A minor is the relative minor of C major. They share the same key signature, no sharps or flats.

Figure 5.1

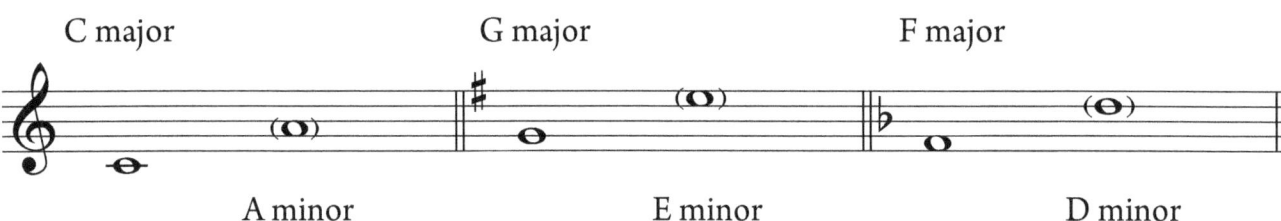

1. For the following examples: Name the major key. Write the tonic of the relative minor with a note in brackets. Name the relative minor key.

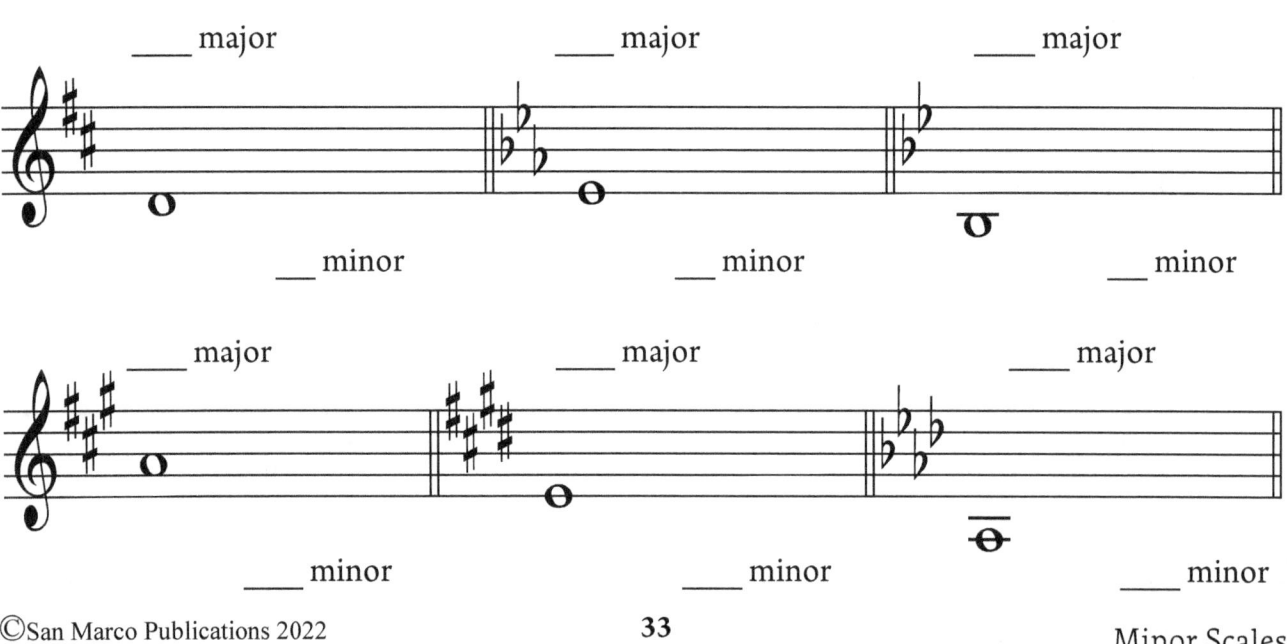

The Circle of Fifths With Minor Keys

Figure 5.2 is the circle of 5ths with added minor keys. The circle of 5ths shows that some of the flat keys sound the same as some of the sharp keys. The key of six flats (E♭minor, G♭major) sounds the same as the key of six sharps (D♯minor, F♯major). Keys which contain the same pitches but are notated differently are called *enharmonic keys* or *enharmonic equivalents*.

Figure 5.2

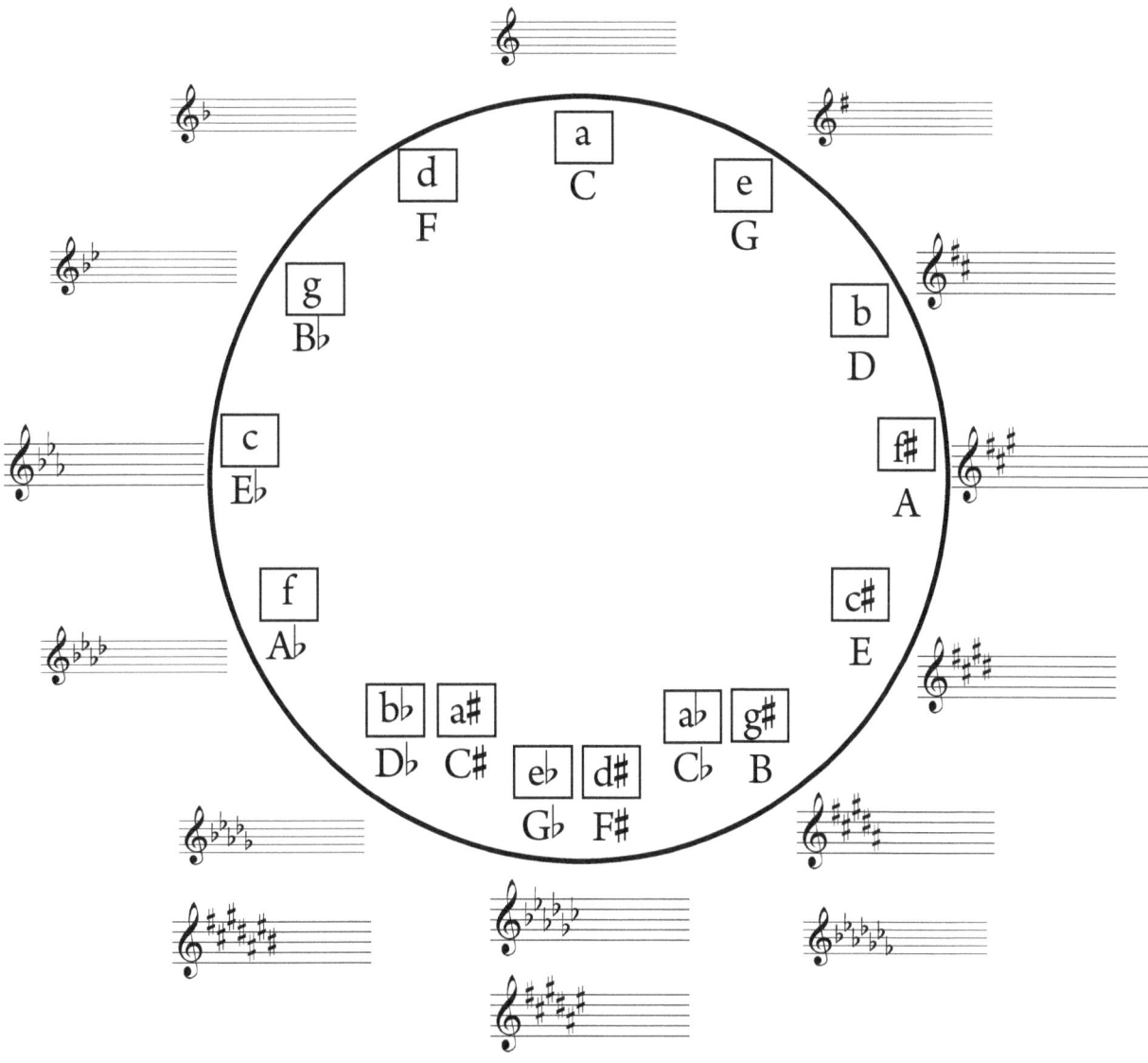

Minor keys are shown with lower case letters.

Minor Scale Review

There are three types of minor scales:

1. **natural minor**: uses the same key signature as its relative major.
2. **harmonic minor**: is the natural minor with $\hat{7}$ raised a half step.
3. **melodic minor**: is the natural minor with $\hat{6}$ and $\hat{7}$ raised a half step ascending, and lowered a half step descending.

Figure 5.3 show all three versions of the D minor scale.

Figure 5.3

D natural minor

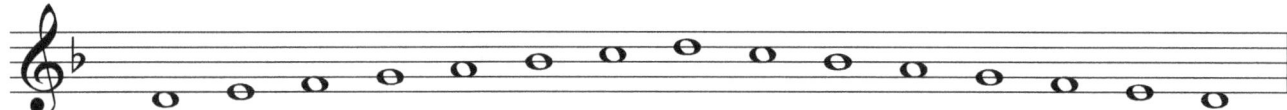

D harmonic minor

D melodic minor

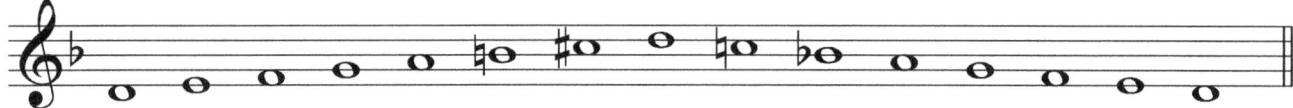

The Leading Tone and the Subtonic

There are two technical names for $\hat{7}$ in minor keys. When $\hat{7}$ is raised and is a half step from the tonic it is called the **leading tone**. In the natural minor and descending melodic minor, where $\hat{7}$ is not raised and is a whole step away from the tonic, it is called the ***subtonic***.

1. Name the key and following scales as natural, harmonic or melodic. e.g. *D harmonic minor.*

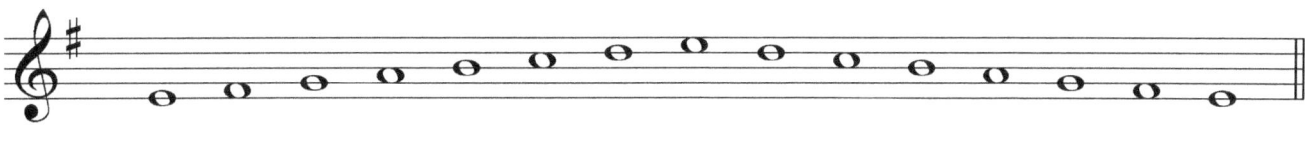

Scale: _____

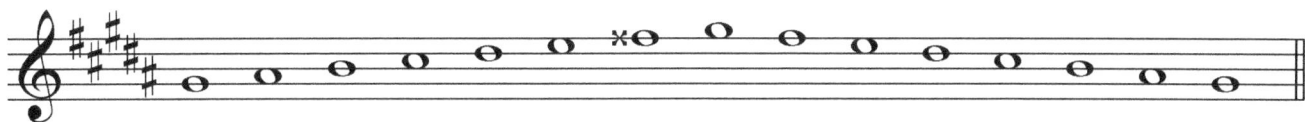

Scale: _____

Scale: _____

Scale: _____

Scale: _____

Scale: _____

Scale: _____

Minor Scales

2. Write the following scales ascending and descending in quarter notes using a key signature.

C# harmonic minor

E♭ melodic minor

D natural minor

F# harmonic minor

C melodic minor

B♭ natural minor

E harmonic minor

Parallel Major and Minor Keys

Major and minor keys that share the same root or tonic are considered *parallel major* and *minor keys*. Sometimes they are called *tonic major and minor*. C major and C minor are parallel major and minor or tonic major and minor. This means that they share the same tonic.

Enharmonic Tonic Major and Minor Keys

Enharmonic major or minor keys are keys with the same tonic that have a different name. For example, C♯ major and D♭ major are enharmonic tonic majors. They are major scales that share the same tonic, but have a different name. C♯ and D♭ are the same note.

The enharmonic tonic minor of G♭ minor is F♯ minor. The same tonic, named differently.

The tonic minor of G♭ major is G♭ minor.
The enharmonic tonic minor of G♭ major is F♯ minor. All this means is that it is the minor scale with the same tonic as G♭ major, but renamed. Its name has been changed enharmonically from G♭ to F♯.

1. Complete the following.

   a. The enharmonic tonic major of C♯ major is _____

   b. The enharmonic tonic minor of B♭ major is _____

   c. The enharmonic tonic major of C♭ major is _____

   d. The parallel minor of D major is _____

   e. The tonic major of G minor is _____

   f. The enharmonic tonic minor of E♭ major is _____

2. Write the following scales ascending and descending in half notes using a key signature.

The harmonic minor scale with the key signature of 4 flats

The melodic minor scale that is the parallel minor of D major

The natural minor scale with G as the subtonic

The harmonic minor scale with A as the leading tone

The melodic minor scale with E♭ as the tonic

The natural minor with G as the supertonic

The enharmonic tonic melodic minor, of D♭ major

6
Intervals

Review

Major intervals are 2, 3, 6, and 7. Perfect intervals are 1, 4, 5, and 8. For an interval to be major or perfect the top note must be a member of the bottom notes major scale.

Figure 6.1 shows the major and perfect intervals formed between the notes of the C major scale.

Figure 6.1

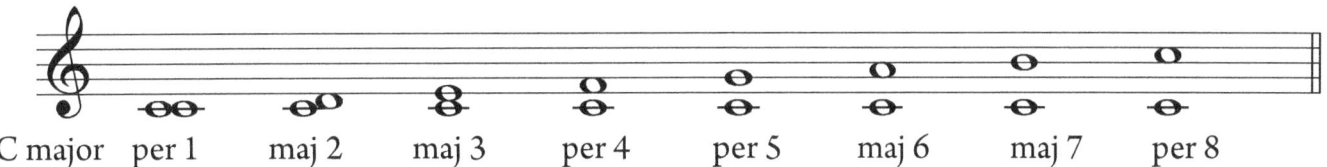

Minor intervals are found only on 2, 3, 6 and 7. They are always a half step smaller or closer together than a major interval that has the same number. A minor 2nd is the smallest interval. A half step is a minor 2nd.

Figure 6.2 illustrates the difference between major and minor intervals. Lowering the top note of a major interval one half step creates a minor interval. Another way to create a minor interval is to raise the bottom note of a major interval one half step. This brings the notes closer together.

Figure 6.2

Accidental Placement

When placing accidentals in front of intervals:

a. For interval numbers from 2 to 6, place the upper accidental closest to the note and the lower accidental to the left.
b. If the two accidentals of a 6th don't collide, they can be aligned vertically.
c. For an interval greater than a 6th, the intervals can align vertically.

Figure 6.3

1. Name the following intervals.

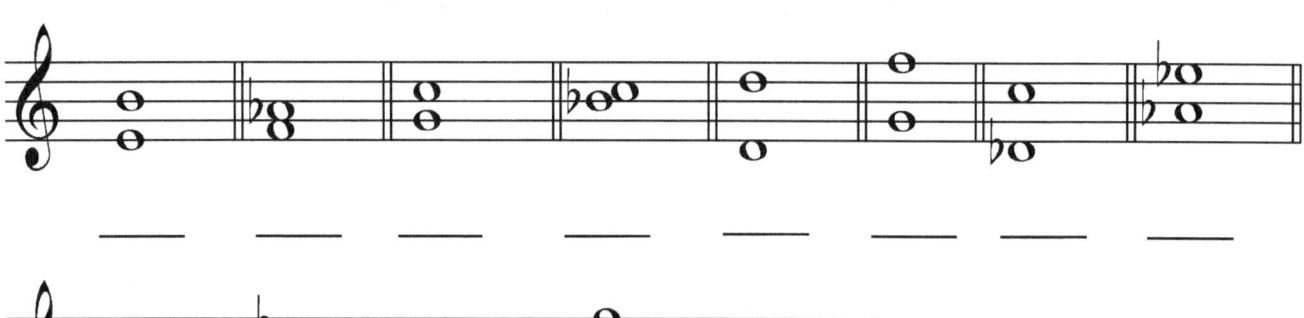

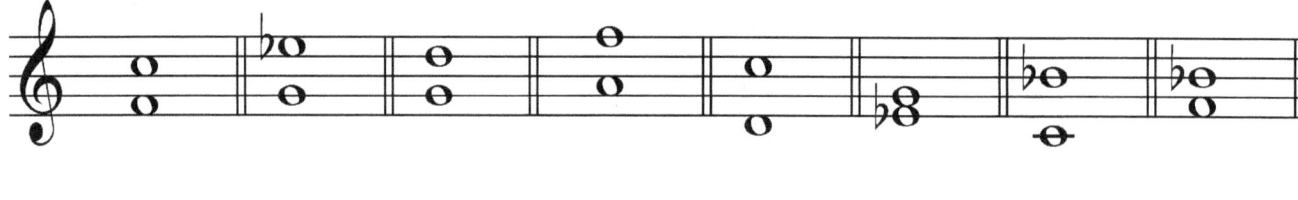

2. Write the following melodic intervals above the given notes.

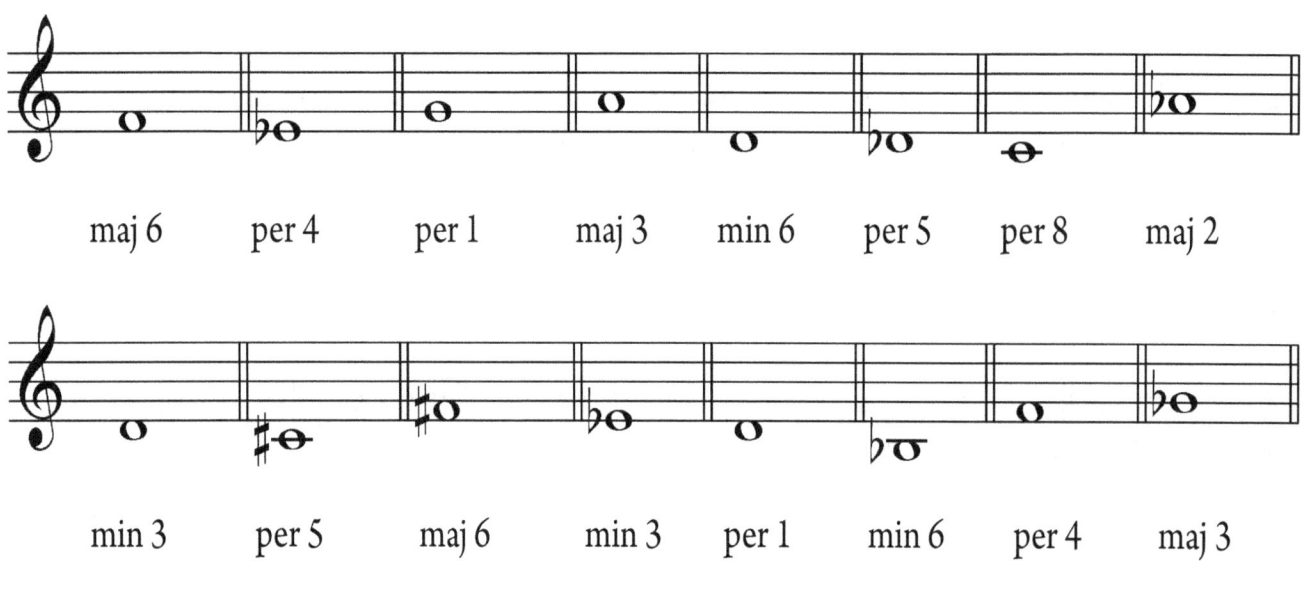

Augmented Intervals

An ***augmented interval*** is an interval that is a half step larger than a perfect or major interval. Another way to look at this is: the notes of the augmented interval are one half step further apart than the notes of a major or perfect interval.

Figure 6.3 shows that raising the top note of a major or perfect interval creates an augmented interval. Compare these intervals with those found in Figure 6.44.

Figure 6.4

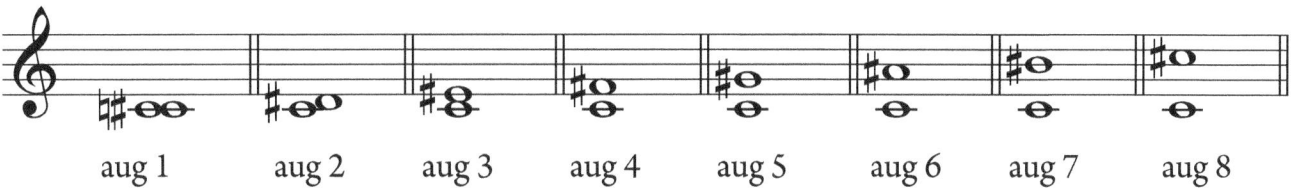

Another way to create an augmented interval is to lower the bottom note one half step. This makes the note one half step further apart and results in an augmented interval.

The intervals in Figure 6.5 are all augmented.

Figure 6.5

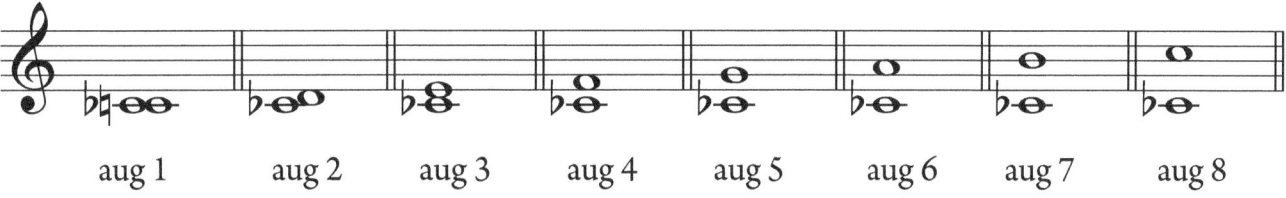

1. The following intervals are major or perfect. In the second measure, rewrite them and change the top note to make them augmented. Name each interval.

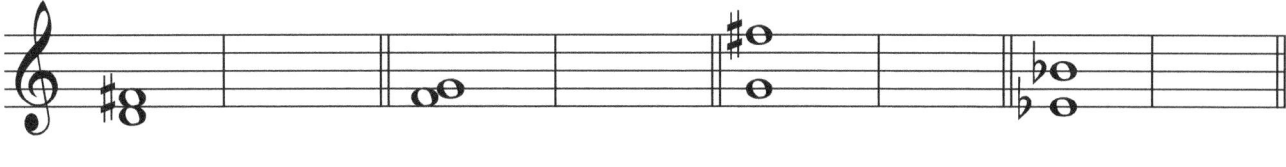

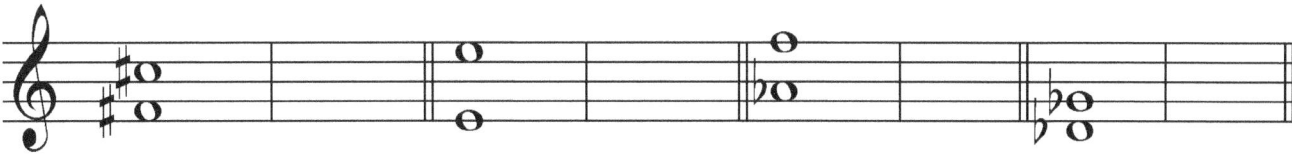

©San Marco Publications 2022

2. The following intervals are major or perfect. In the second measure, rewrite them and change the bottom note to make them augmented. Name each interval.

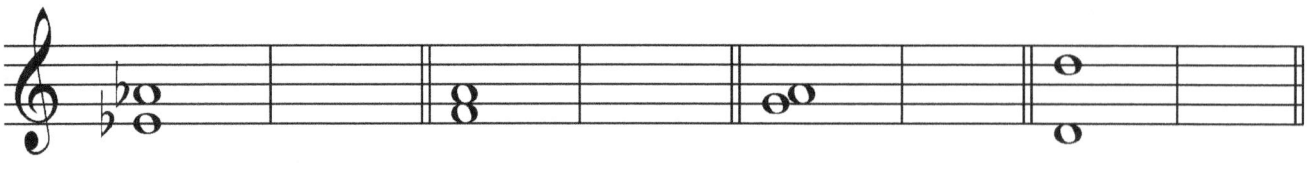

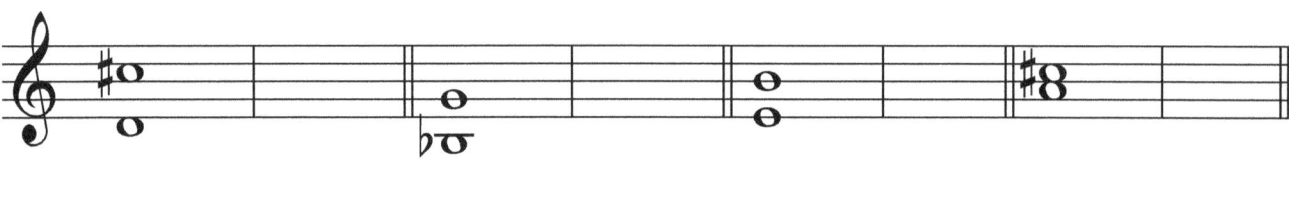

3. Write the following melodic intervals above the given notes.

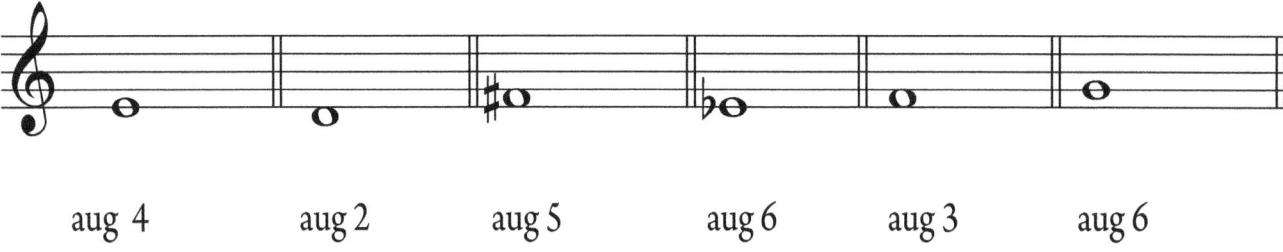

aug 4   aug 2   aug 5   aug 6   aug 3   aug 6

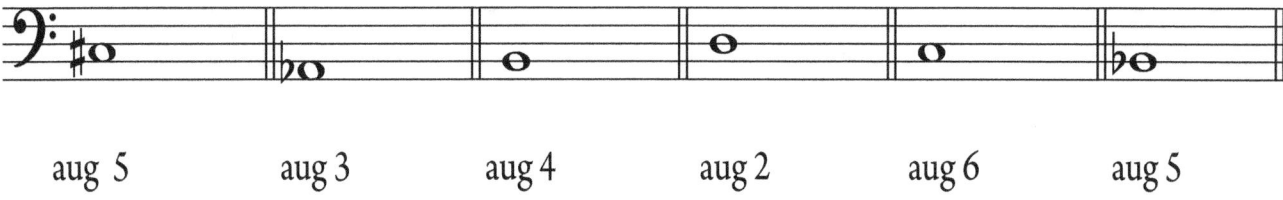

aug 5   aug 3   aug 4   aug 2   aug 6   aug 5

Diminished Intervals

A *diminished interval* is one half step smaller than a perfect interval. Lowering the top note or raising the bottom note of a perfect interval one half step results in a diminished interval.

Figure 6.6 contains diminished intervals.

Figure 6.6

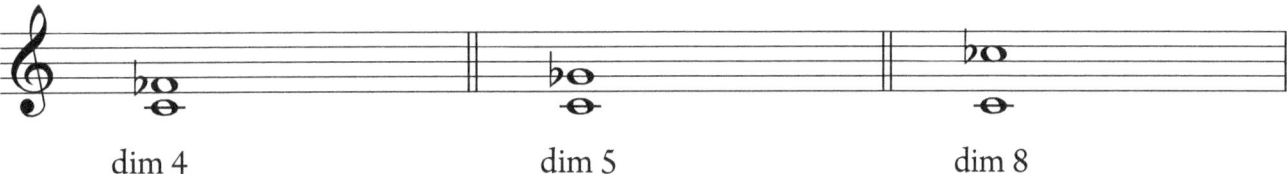

When the top note of a major interval is lowered one half step it becomes minor. When it is lowered two half steps the interval becomes diminished.

Figure 6.7 shows these interval relationships.

Figure 6.7

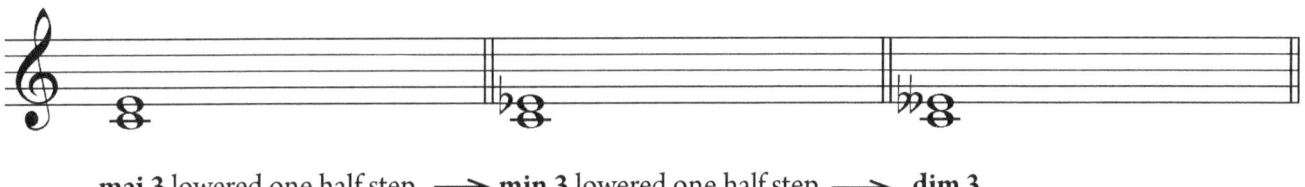

A major interval can be made diminished by raising the bottom note two half steps. Raising the bottom note brings the notes closer together.

Figure 6.8 shows that raising the bottom note of a major 3rd one half step produces a minor 3rd. Raising it two half steps produces a diminished 3rd.

Figure 6.8

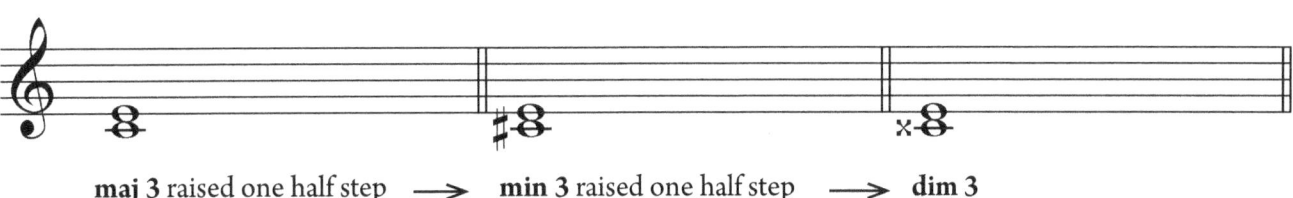

Intervals are always solved using the bottom note as the key note. This is true even if the bottom note comes after the top note in a melodic interval.

In Figure 6.9 both intervals are a minor 6th. The lowest note in the second interval comes after the highest note but the interval is still a minor 6th.

Figure 6.9

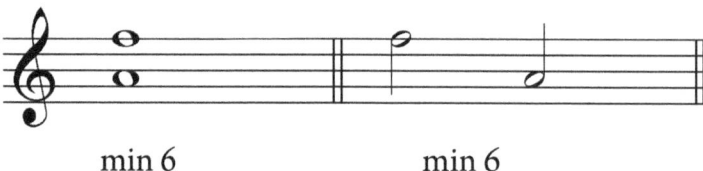

We consider the perfect unison the smallest interval, even though a unison is not really an interval. An interval is defined as the distance between two notes. There is no distance between the notes of a unison.

The unison requires special consideration. Since there is no distance between the notes of a unison, it cannot be made smaller. Unisons can never be diminished intervals. If any note of a unison is altered, the notes become further away from each other, and it becomes augmented.
Study Figure 6.10.

Figure 6.10

This chart shows the relationship between intervals. The arrow indicates the movement of one half step.

diminished ← minor ← **major** → augmented

diminshed ← **perfect** → augmented

The intervals in each measure of Figure 6.11 sound exactly the same, but are named differently. The top note in example a) is changed enharmonically from B♭ to A♯, and the bottom note in example b) is changed enharmonically from A♭ to G♯. Even though the pitch does not change, the interval number and quality changes.

Figure 6.11

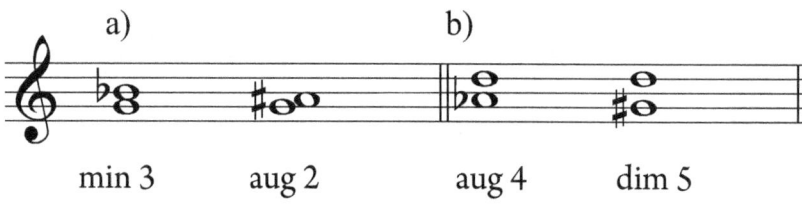

©San Marco Publications 2022

1. The following intervals are major or perfect. In the second measure, rewrite them and change the top note to make them diminished. Name each interval.

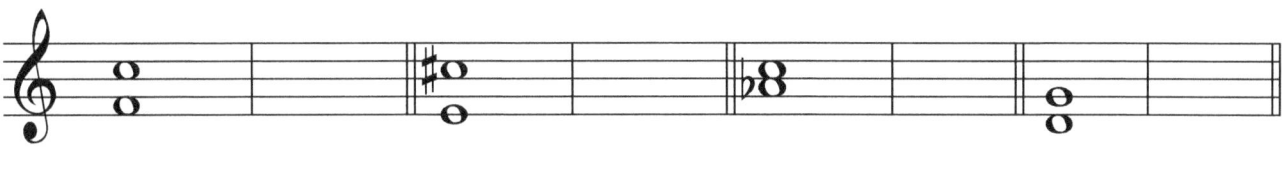

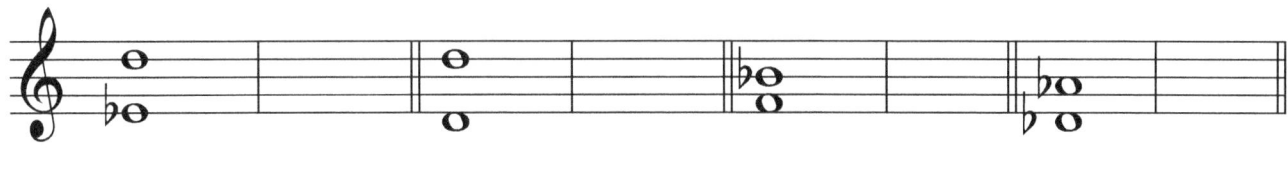

2. The following intervals are major or perfect. In the second measure, rewrite them and change the bottom note to make them diminished. Name each interval.

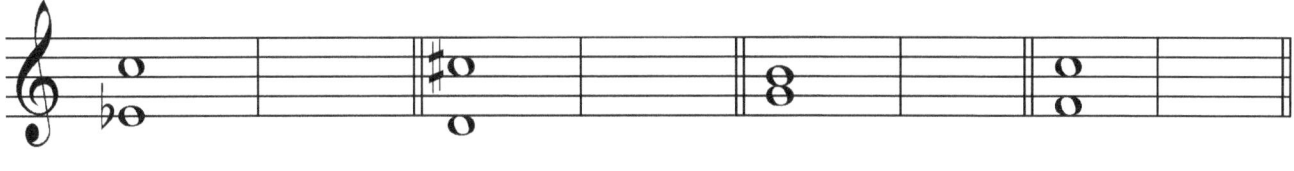

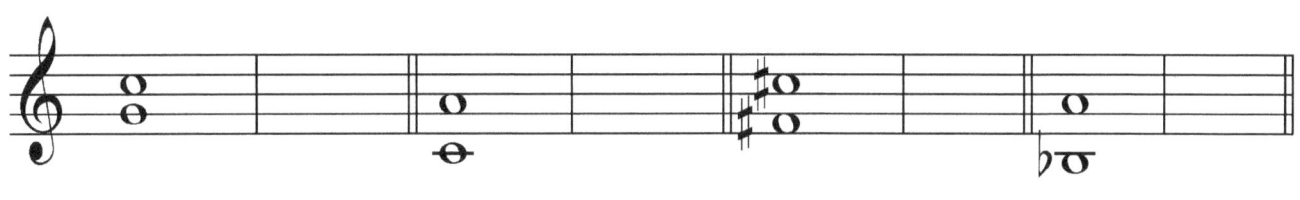

3. Write the following melodic intervals above the given notes.

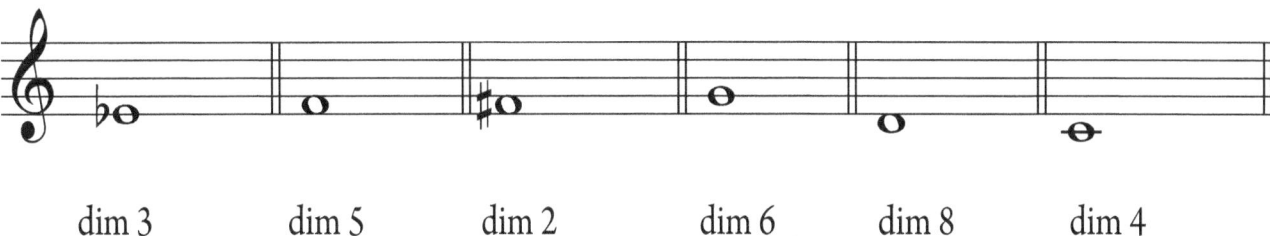

dim 3   dim 5   dim 2   dim 6   dim 8   dim 4

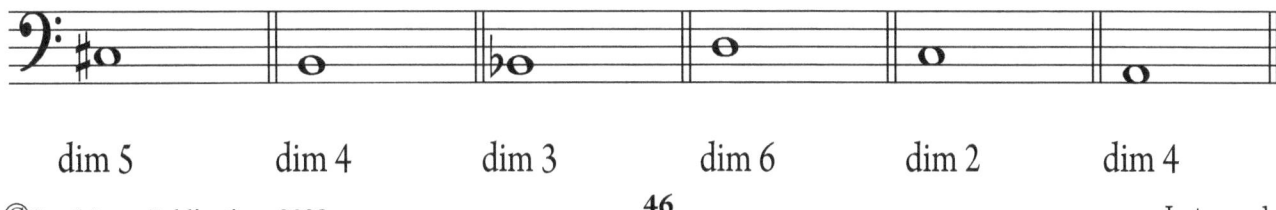

dim 5   dim 4   dim 3   dim 6   dim 2   dim 4

4. Name the following intervals.

5. Name the following melodic intervals.

Frederic Chopin
Ballade, Op 23, No. 1

6. Write the following melodic intervals.

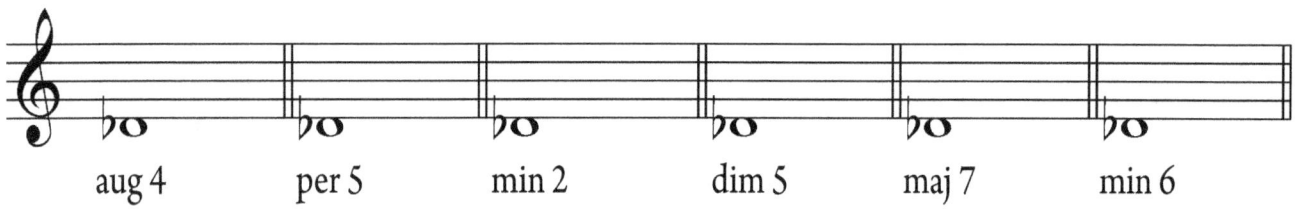

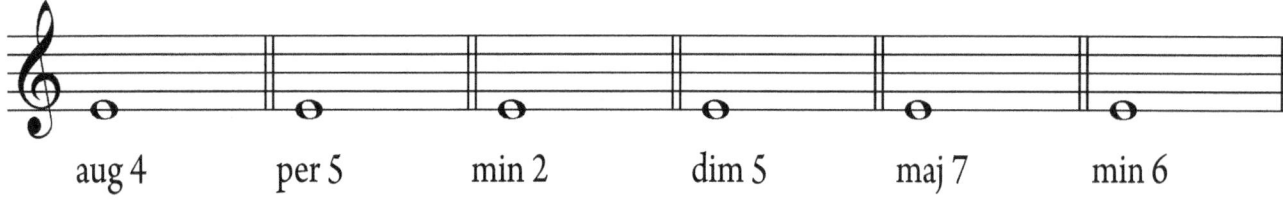

Solving Unusual Intervals

Sometimes the bottom note of an interval is not the tonic of a logical major key.

The lowest note in the interval in Figure 6.12 is a D♯. D♯ is not the tonic of a major key.

Figure 6.12

? 3

To solve this interval:
1. Since both notes have the same accidental, a sharp, remove both sharps (Figure 6.13).
2. With the sharps removed the bottom note is now D, a logical key.
3. The interval D to F is a minor 3rd. Since D♯ to F♯ is the same distance a half step higher, it is also a minor 3rd. The interval number and quality is the same with the added sharps. D♭ to F♭ is also a minor 3rd, being a half step lower than D to F. The movement up or down by half step does not change the interval quality.

Figure 6.13

min 3   min 3   min 3

The interval in Figure 6.14a has an A♯ as its lowest note. We know this interval is a 4th since the letter names are A to D (A-B-C-D = 1-2-3-4). A♯ is not the tonic of a major key. By lowering it a half step to A♮, we have the tonic of logical key (A major). Since we lowered the bottom note one half step, we must lower the top note one half step. D becomes D♭. A to D♭ is a dim 4th. Therefore, A♯ to D is also a dim 4th.

Figure 6.14b contains F♭ as its lowest note. When we raise it one half step, we get a logical major key, F major. Since we raised the bottom note a half step, we must raise the top note a half step from D to D♯. F to D♯ is the interval of an aug 6th. Therefore, F♭ to D is also an aug 6th.

Figure 6.14

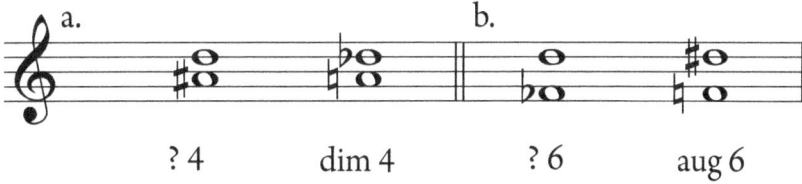

? 4   dim 4   ? 6   aug 6

1. Name the following intervals.

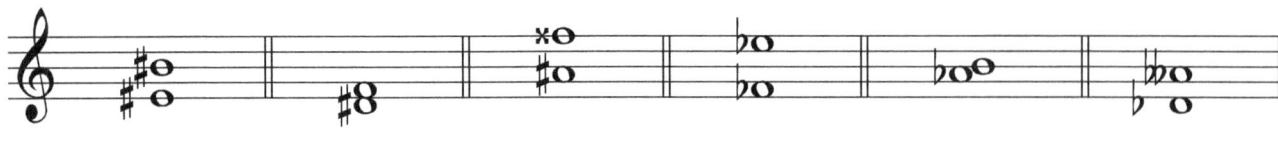

2. Name the following intervals.

3. Rewrite the above intervals changing the upper note enharmonically. Rename them.

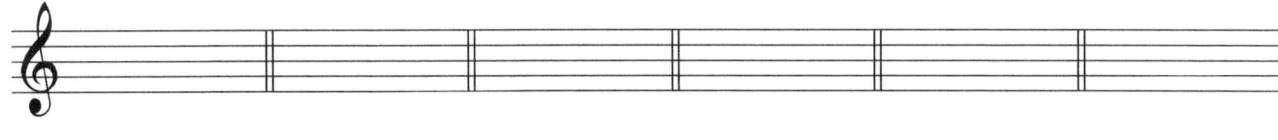

4. Name the intervals under the brackets.

Felix Mendelssohn
Trio in C minor

Antonin Dvorak
Trio in F minor, II

Ludwig van Beethoven
Symphony No. 9. III

Johann Sebastian Bach
Sonata No. 1 in B minor

Intervals

7
Chords

Major and Minor Triads

Triads consist of a root, third and fifth played together. The interval quality of the third and fifth determine the triad quality.

Figure 7.1 contains a C major and a C minor triad. The **major triad** consists of the intervals of a major 3rd and perfect 5th above the root. The **minor triad** consists of the intervals of a minor 3rd and a perfect 5th above the root.

Figure 7.1

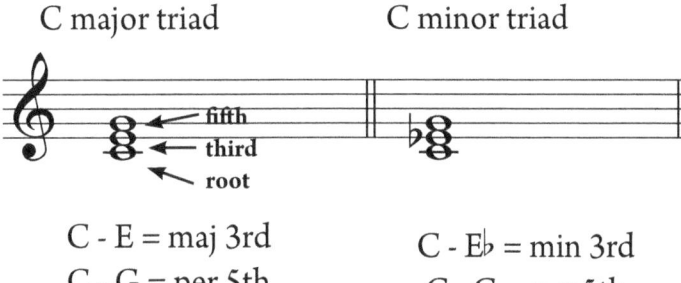

1. Name the following triads as major or minor.

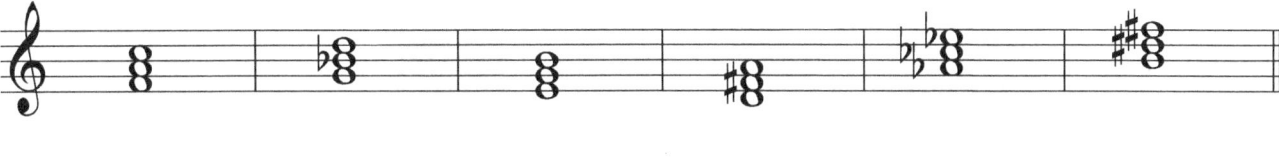

Triad Inversions

Triads can occur in three positions.

1. **Root position** occurs when the root of the triad is the lowest note.
2. **First inversion** occurs when the 3rd of the triad is the lowest note.
3. **Second inversion** occurs when the 5th of the triad is the lowest note.

Figure 7.2 shows the three positions of the D major triad. The chords have been named in two ways. The root/quality symbol for the D major triad in root position is **D**. First inversion is **D/F♯**. This means that it is the D major triad with F♯ as the lowest note. Second inversion is **D/A**. This means that it is the D major triad with A as the lowest note. This method of naming chords is common in popular music. The formula for this is triad/bass note.

Roman numerals under the triad are called functional chord symbols. The functional chord symbol for the tonic triad in D major is **I**. The functional chord symbol for the tonic triad in D major in first inversion is **I^6**. "I" indicates that it is the triad built on $\hat{1}$ in D major and the "6" indicates that it is in first inversion. The origin of the 6 comes from the interval of a 6th between the lowest note F♯ and the highest note D in the triad. The functional chord symbol for the tonic triad in second inversion is **I$^6_4$**. This indicates the intervals of a 6th (A to F) and a 4th (A to D) above the lowest note of the triad. In all three cases, the uppercase Roman numeral "I" means it is a major triad built on scale degree $\hat{1}$ of the key. Major triads use uppercase Roman numerals.

Figure 7.2

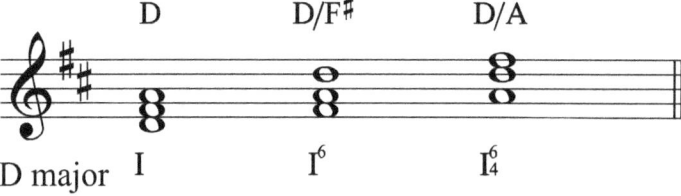

D major   I   I^6 I$^6_4$

Figure 7.3 illustrates the chord symbols for the E minor triad in root position and inversions. In root/quality chord symbols, minor triads are indicated with an "m" beside the uppercase letter. In functional chord symbols, minor triads are shown with a lower case Roman numeral.

Figure 7.3

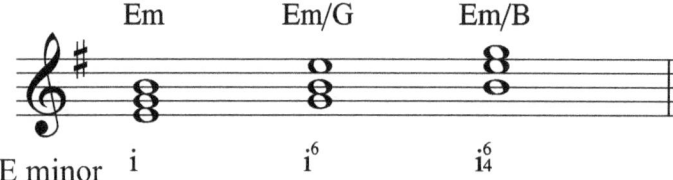

E minor   i   i^6 i$^6_4$

Solving Triads

Figure 7.4

Solving a triad involves stating its root, quality and position. To solve the triad in Figure 7.4:

1. If it is not in root position, put it into root position. Figure 7.5 shows us that the root is: **E**.

Figure 7.5

2. Determine the intervals between the root and 3rd and the root and 5th. In Figure 7.6 E to G♯ is a major 3rd and E to B is a perfect 5th making its quality **major**.

Figure 7.6

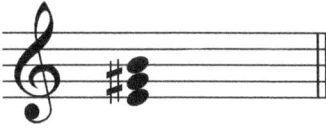

3. Examine the lowest note of the given triad. In Figure 7.4 it is the 3rd, G♯. When the 3rd is the lowest note, the position of the triad is **first inversion**. This triad is solved as follows:

> Root: E
> Quality: major
> Position: 1st inversion

1. Name the root of the following triads.

2. Solve the following triads by stating the root, quality, and position. Add root/quality chord symbols to each.

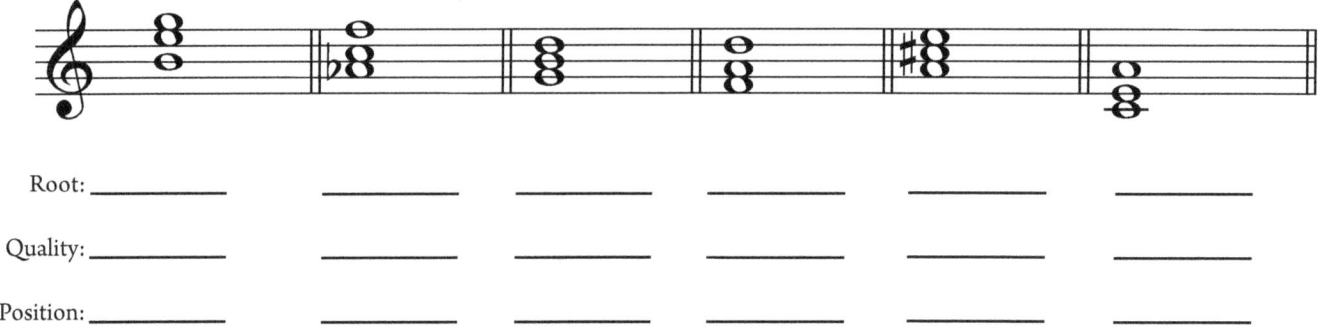

Root: _____   _____   _____   _____   _____   _____

Quality: _____   _____   _____   _____   _____   _____

Position: _____   _____   _____   _____   _____   _____

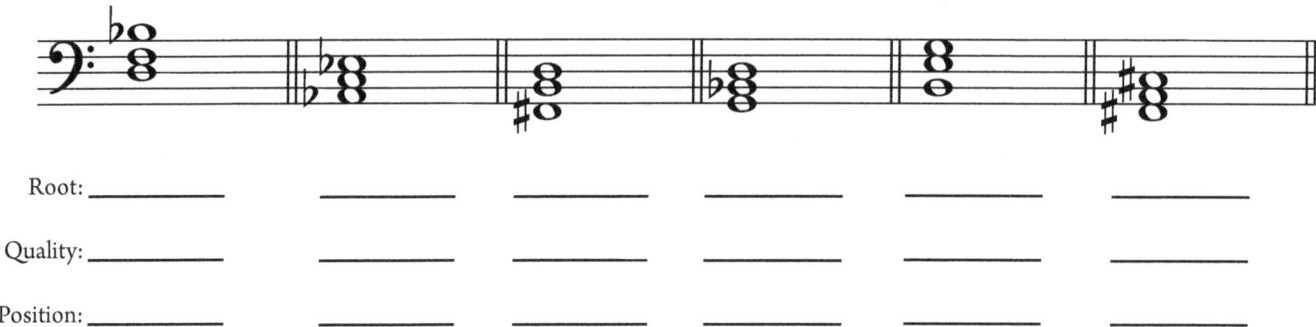

Root: _____   _____   _____   _____   _____   _____

Quality: _____   _____   _____   _____   _____   _____

Position: _____   _____   _____   _____   _____   _____

Triads Built on the Major and Minor Scale

Figure 7.7 illustrates the major and minor triads that occur on notes in the scale of C major. Each triad can be named for the scale degree it is built upon. The triad built on $\hat{1}$, the tonic, is considered the **tonic triad** in C major. The triad built on $\hat{2}$, the supertonic, is considered the **supertonic triad** in C major. The triad built on $\hat{3}$ is the **mediant triad**, etc.

Figure 7.7

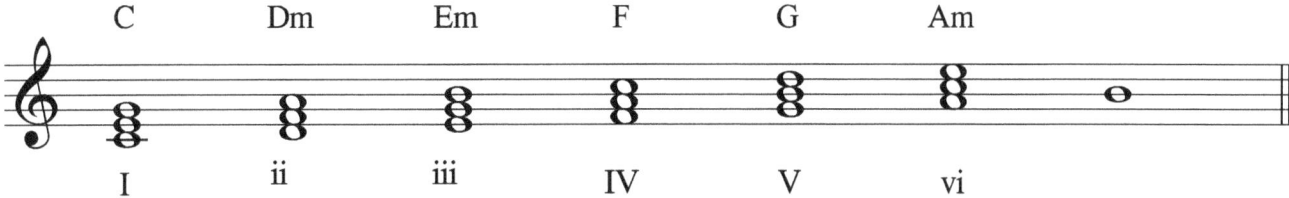

Both major and minor triads occur in the harmonic minor scale. Figure 7.8 shows the triads on the A harmonic minor scale. Major triads occur on the dominant ($\hat{5}$) and the submediant ($\hat{6}$). Minor triads occur on the tonic ($\hat{1}$) and subdominant ($\hat{4}$).

Any triads not shown have qualities other than major and minor and will be studied later.

Figure 7.8

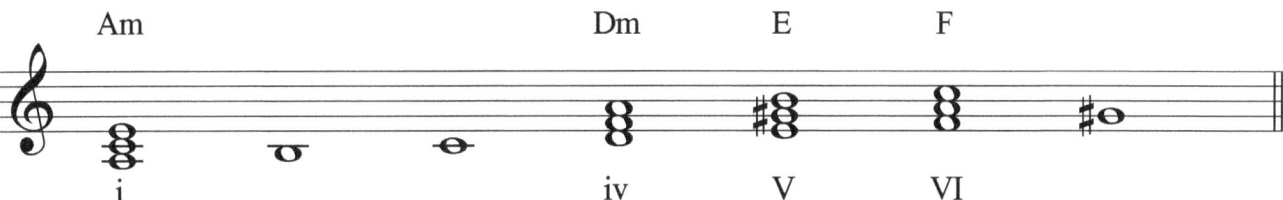

1. Write triads on the scale degrees indicated. Add root/quality and functional chord symbols.

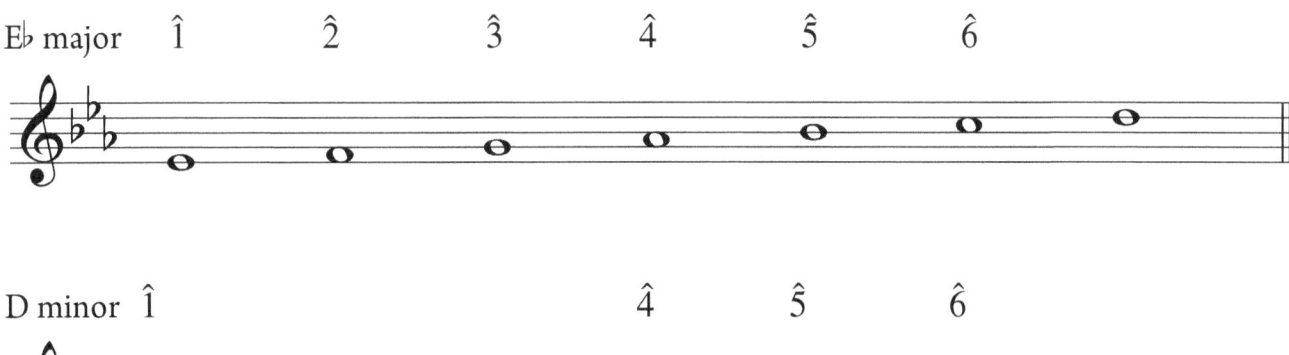

2. Write the following triads using a key signature for each. Write the functional chord symbol.

| The mediant triad in F major | The dominant triad in C minor | The supertonic triad in B♭ major | The submediant triad in D minor |

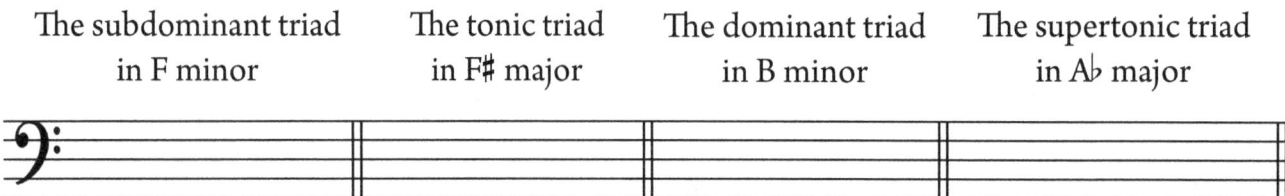

| The subdominant triad in F minor | The tonic triad in F♯ major | The dominant triad in B minor | The supertonic triad in A♭ major |

3. Write the following triads using accidentals instead of a key signature. Write the root/quality chord symbol.

   a) the tonic triad of G minor in second inversion
   b) the supertonic triad of D major in root position
   c) the submediant triad of E minor in first inversion
   d) the dominant triad of C♯ minor in root position
   e) the mediant triad of E♭ major in first inversion
   f) the subdominant triad of F♯ minor in second inversion

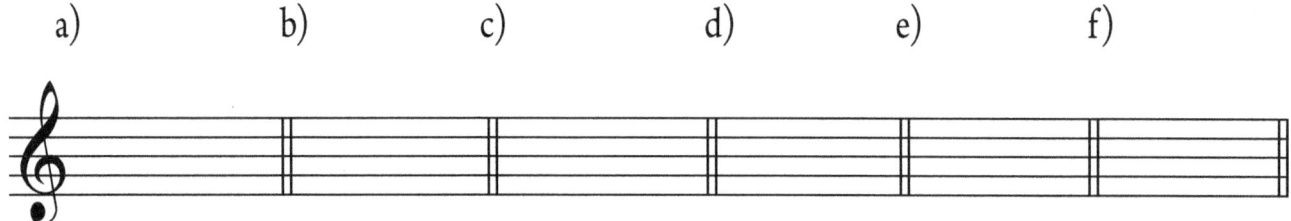

©San Marco Publications 2022 — Chords

Triads in Open Position

So far, we have studied triads in ***close position.*** Close position occurs when the notes of the triad are as close together as possible. Triads may also be written in ***open position.*** In open position, the notes of the triad are spaced out over more than one octave. Often one of the notes of the triad is written more than once or ***doubled.*** The most common note to double is the root. The lowest note of the triad determines the position of the triad no matter in what order the other notes appear. Figure 7.9 shows different positions of the D minor triad in open position.

Figure 7.9

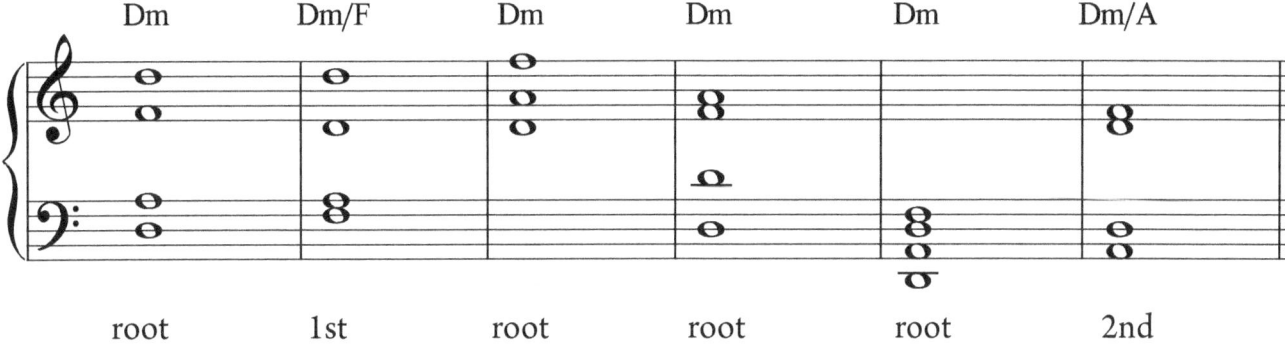

1. State the root, quality and position of the following triads.

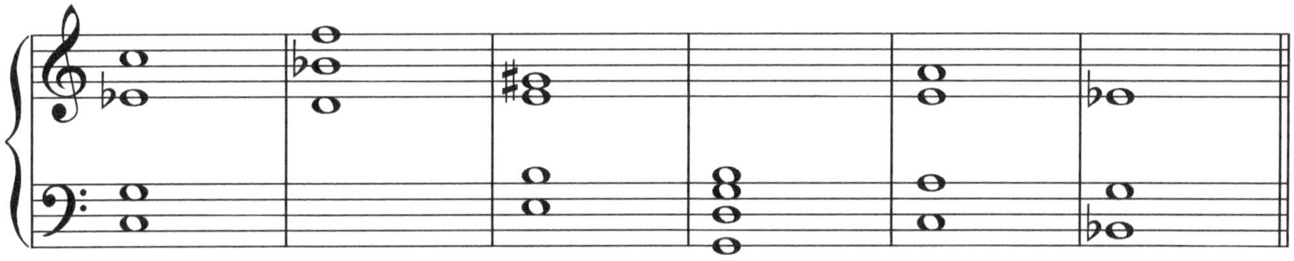

root: _____ _____ _____ _____ _____ _____
quality: _____ _____ _____ _____ _____ _____
position: _____ _____ _____ _____ _____ _____

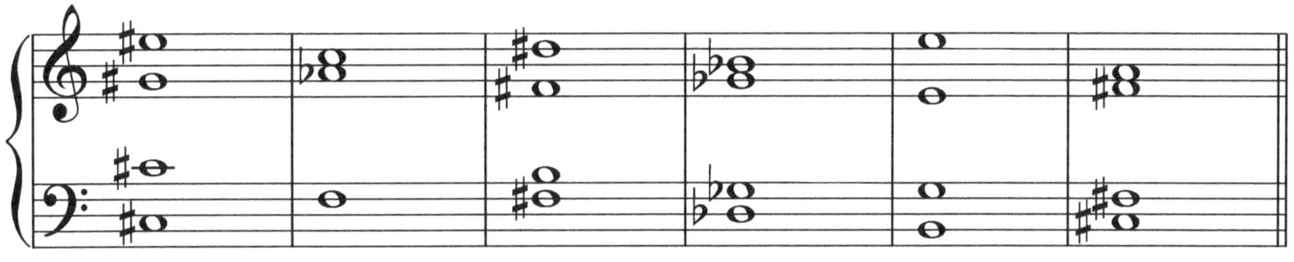

root: _____ _____ _____ _____ _____ _____
quality: _____ _____ _____ _____ _____ _____
position: _____ _____ _____ _____ _____ _____

The Dominant Seventh Chord

Seventh chords are very common in Western music and we hear them all the time.

One of the most common seventh chords is the **dominant seventh.** The functional chord symbol for the dominant seventh is V^7. This means that the chord is built on scale degree $\hat{5}$ (the dominant) and there is the interval of a seventh above the root of the chord. It contains four notes: the root, the 3rd, the 5th and the 7th. V^7 is a major triad with a minor 7th above the root. In other words, the intervals above the root are a major 3rd, perfect 5th and a minor 7th.

Figure 7.10 contains the dominant triad and the dominant seventh chord in C major. The root/quality chord symbol for V^7 is G^7.

Figure 7.10

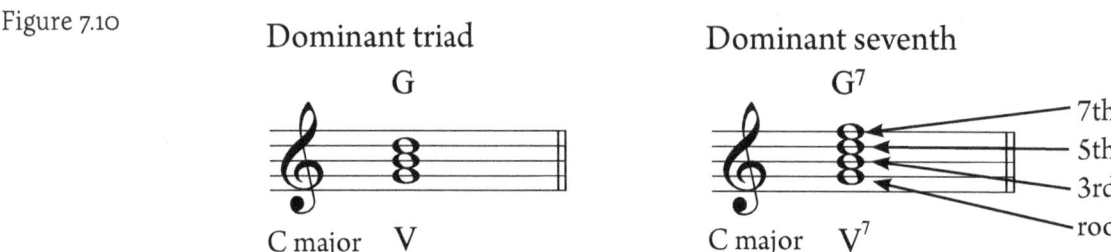

V^7 contains certain notes, like the leading tone, which pull our ear toward the tonic chord.

Figure 7.11 shows V^7 chords in C and G major and D and E minor. When we use a key signature for these chords, the seventh of V^7 is automatically a minor seventh. In minor keys V^7, like V needs a raised $\hat{7}$.

Figure 7.11

The dominant seventh sounds the same in tonic major and minor keys.

Figure 7.12 show the dominant seventh chords in F major and F minor. Even though the notation is different they sound the same and are made up of the same notes.

Figure 7.12

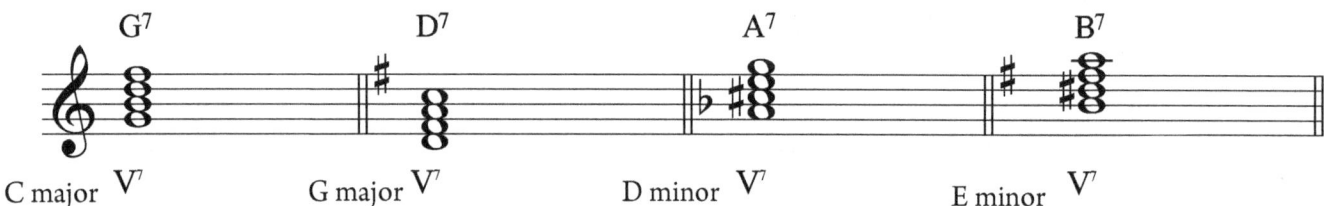

1. Name the key and write the functional and root/quality chord symbols for the following dominant seventh chords.

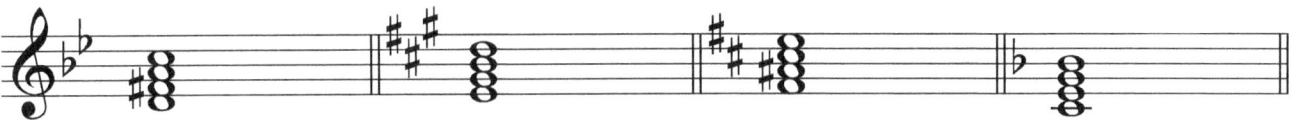

2. The following dominant 7ths are written in open position without key signatures. Name the two keys where each one may be found.

key: _____ _____ _____ _____ _____ _____

key: _____ _____ _____ _____ _____ _____

A Note About Terminology

The leading tone is the seventh degree of the scale. It may also be referred to as scale degree 7 ($\hat{7}$). We don't call the leading tone the "seventh." It is considered the *leading tone* or *scale degree seven* ($\hat{7}$). The word "seventh" is the term reserved to indicate the seventh of a seventh chord. In this case the word seventh may also be abbreviated to "7th."

The dominant 7th chord in C major is GBDF. F is the 7th of this chord. B, the 3rd of this chord, is the leading tone or scale degree $\hat{7}$ in C major. B is not called the *7th of C major*. The word "*seventh*" is reserved to indicate the 7th of a 7th chord.

1. Name the major key of the following dominant 7th chords.

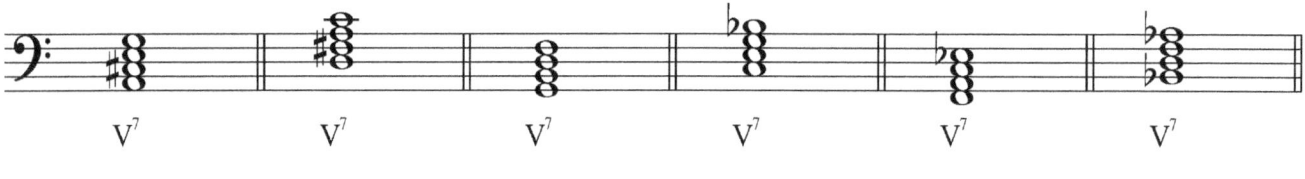

2. Each note below is the root of a dominant 7th chord. Build a dominant 7th chord above each by writing a major 3rd, perfect 5th and minor 7th above the root. Add the root/quality chord symbols above each chord.

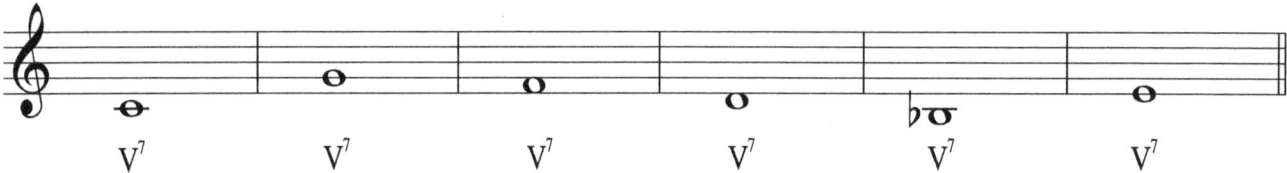

3. Write dominant 7th chords for the following keys. Use a key signature for each.

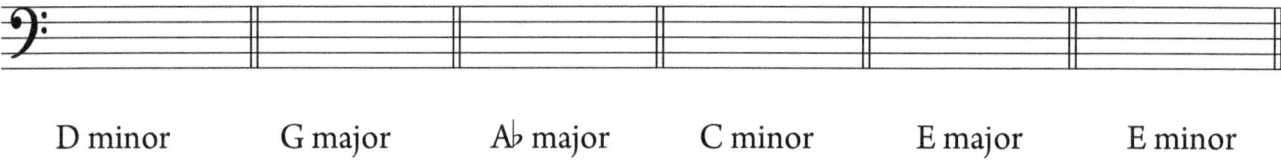

    D minor   G major   A♭ major   C minor   E major   E minor

4. Write dominant 7th chords using a key signature according to the root/quality chord symbols. Name the **major key** for each.

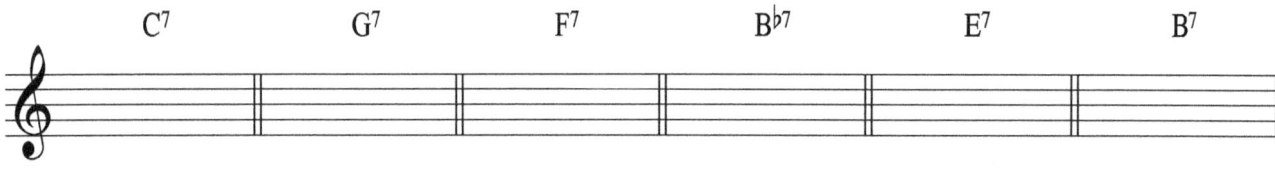

Chordal Texture in a Musical Score

Composers use chords in many different textures when writing a musical score. This depends on the style, type of composition, instruments, or performers needed to bring the score to life.

Figure 7.13 is the opening of "Hallelujah Chorus" from Handel's Messiah covered in Level 5. This work is written for a 4 voice choir. The four voices work together and create chords as they sing. The staff under the score is added here to show the chords that are formed when the choir sings together. On this staff, the chords are reduced to their simplest form. The bass voice, which is the lowest note, determines the inversion of the chord.

Figure 7.13

Figure 7.14 contains a left hand accompaniment of broken triads. The first 2 measures contain the tonic triad in G major in root position. Measure 3 is the subdominant triad in 2nd inversion.

Figure 7.14

In Figure 7.15 the left hand is made up of extended broken D♭ major chords.

Figure 7.15

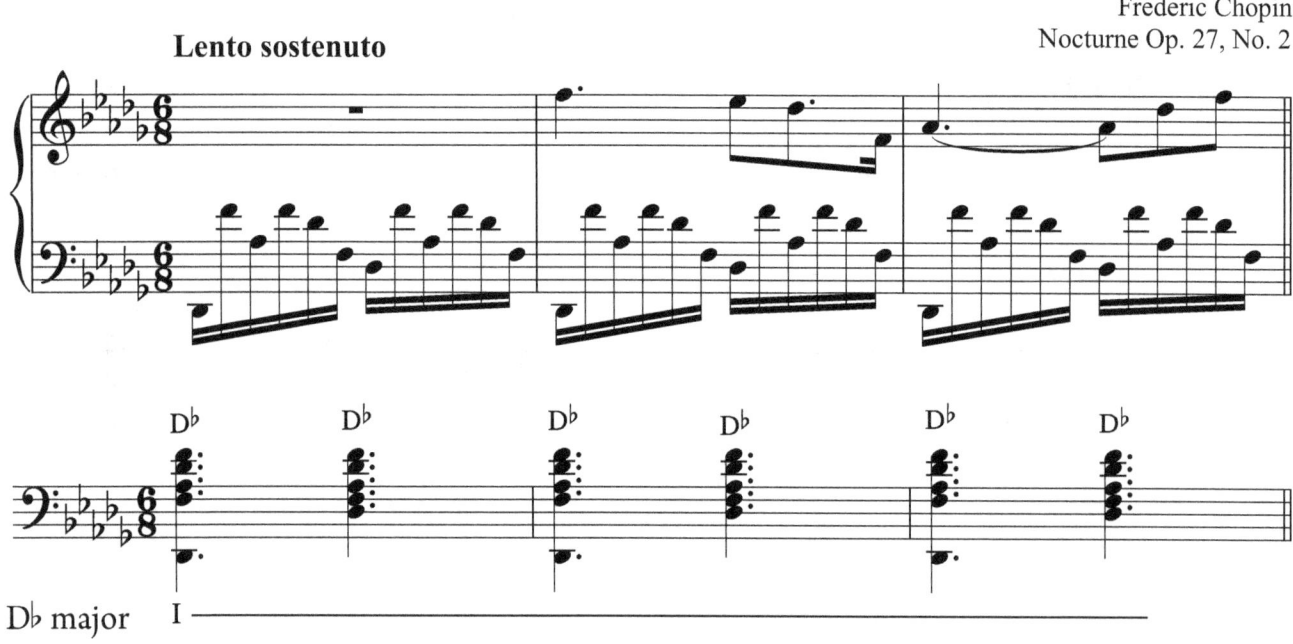

1. For the following musical examples: Name the key. For each outlined chord, state the root, type, position and scale degree on which the chord is built.

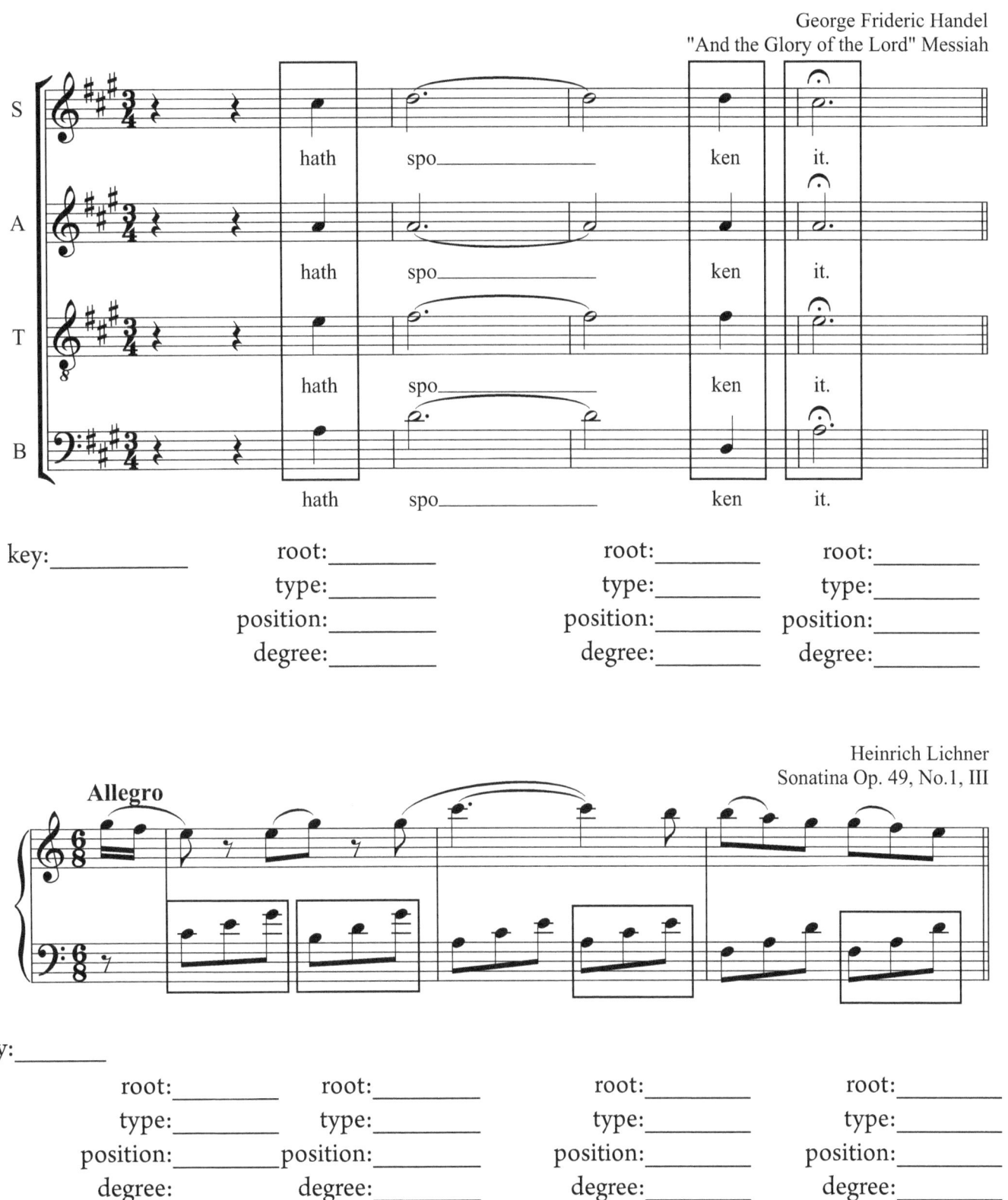

key:_____   root:_____   root:_____   root:_____
                 type:_____   type:_____   type:_____
                 position:_____ position:_____ position:_____
                 degree:_____ degree:_____ degree:_____

key:_____
         root:_____   root:_____   root:_____   root:_____
         type:_____   type:_____   type:_____   type:_____
         position:_____ position:_____ position:_____ position:_____
         degree:_____ degree:_____ degree:_____ degree:_____

©San Marco Publications 2022   Chords

Jiri Benda
Sonatina

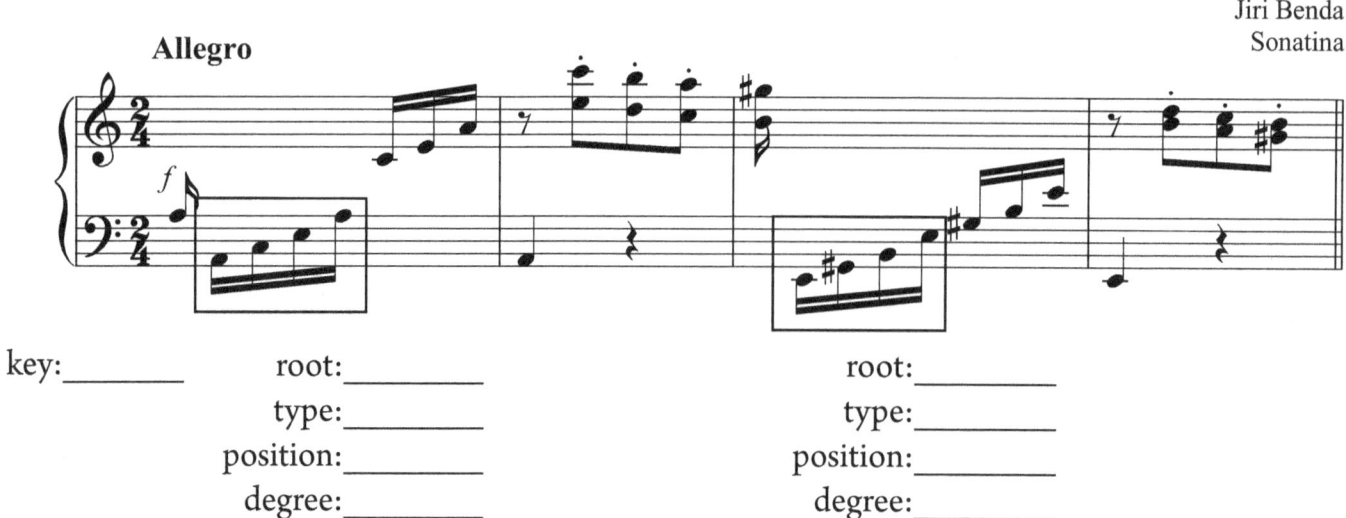

key:_____   root:_____   root:_____
              type:_____   type:_____
              position:_____   position:_____
              degree:_____   degree:_____

Muzio Clementi
Sonatina Op. 36, No. 2

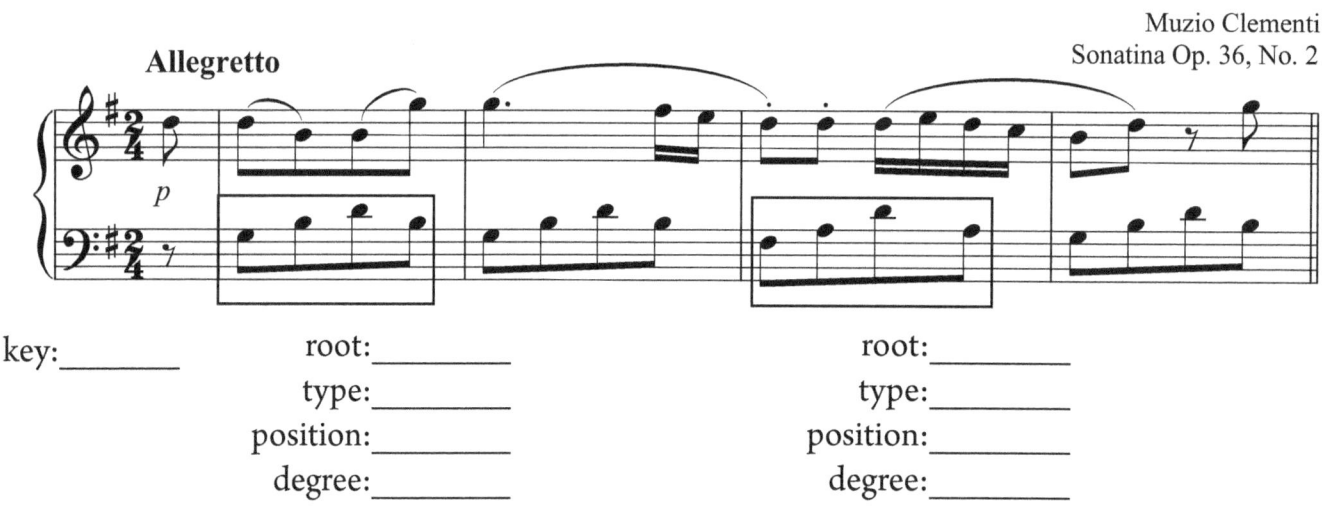

key:_____   root:_____   root:_____
              type:_____   type:_____
              position:_____   position:_____
              degree:_____   degree:_____

Johann Sebastian Bach
Little Prelude VI

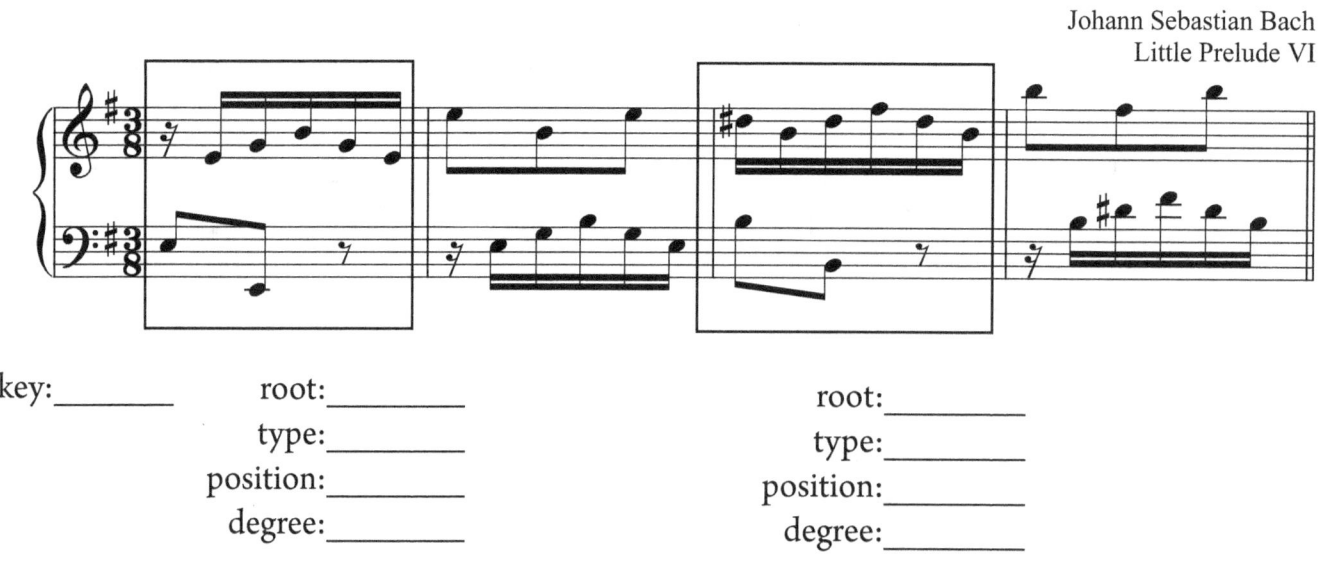

key:_____   root:_____   root:_____
              type:_____   type:_____
              position:_____   position:_____
              degree:_____   degree:_____

©San Marco Publications 2022

Chords

8
History 2

Brandenburg Concerto No. 5 - Johann Sebastian Bach

The six Brandenburg Concerti, BWV 1046-1051, by Johann Sebastian Bach is a collection of chamber music works presented to Christian Ludwig, the Margrave of Brandenburg in 1721. Margrave is a title that used to be given to Governors of German provinces.

He assembled these six *concerti grossi* and presented them, as a type of job application, to the Margrave. A **concerto grosso** is a baroque work for orchestra. It usually has three movements and contains a group of solo instruments called the **concertino** that contrasts with the full string orchestra which is known as the ***ripieno***.

Bach's title for these works was "concertos for a variety of instruments," since each one uses a different combination of instruments. He tried to use as many different combinations of common instruments as he could. Bach never actually called them the Brandenburg Concertos. The name was given to the pieces by a biographer after his death.

The Fifth Concerto in D major for **violin, flute**, and **harpsichord** makes use of a very popular chamber music ensemble (violin, flute, and harpsichord). These three instruments are the *concertino*. Bach, himself a keyboard virtuoso, included an amazing solo harpsichord cadenza in this concerto.
The first movement of this concerto is in ***ritornello*** form. In this form, a repeated section of music, known as the ritornello alternates with different musical sections.

Figure 8.1 is the opening of the Brandenburg Concerto No. 5. by J.S. Bach. The score below is an *open score*. In open score, each instrument has its part written on a separate staff. Traditionally the instrument names are written in Italian and appear on the left of the score from highest to lowest. On this score, the top line is the flute, and the bottom is the harpsichord, with the string section between them.

Figure 8.1

Music Terms

Study the following music terms

ad libitum, ad lib	at the liberty of the performer
alla, all'	in the manner of
animato	animated
loco	return to the normal register
ma	but
meno	less
meno mosso	less motion or movement
non	not
piu	more
piu mosso	more movement
poco a poco	little by little
primo, prima	first, the upper part of a duet
quasi	almost, as if

Review 2

1. Write the following scales ascending and descending in half notes using a key signature.

F# major

The relative minor of F# major, harmonic form

The parallel natural minor of F# major

The enharmonic tonic major of F# major

D melodic minor

G# melodic minor

B♭ harmonic minor

2. Name the intervals under the brackets.

3. Name the root, quality and position of the following chords.

root: _____ _____ _____ _____ _____ _____
quality: _____ _____ _____ _____ _____ _____
position: _____ _____ _____ _____ _____ _____

4. Match the Italian term with its definition.

   a. *poco a poco*   ____return to the normal register

   b. *quasi*   ____but

   c. *alla, all'*   ____less

   d. *piu*   ____less motion or movement

   e. *primo, prima*   ____not

   f. *animato*   ____at the liberty of the performer

   g. *meno*   ____in the manner of

   h. *ad libitum, ad lib*   ____animated

   i. *meno mosso*   ____more

   j. *piu mosso*   ____more movement

   k. *loco*   ____little by little

   l. *non*   ____first, the upper part of a duet

   m. *ma*   ____almost, as if

5. Answer the following questions.

   a. Who composed Brandenburg Concerto No. 5? _____

   b. What genre is this work? _____

   c. What 3 instruments are featured in this work? _____

   d. What is this group of instruments called? _____

   e. The full string orchestra in a concerto grosso is called a

   ☐ripieno   ☐concertino   ☐oratorio   ☐sequence

   f. The form of the first movement of Brandenburg Concerto No. 5 is

   ☐rondo   ☐ritornello   ☐sonata   ☐binary

9
Cadences

Music is divided into sections or units of various lengths called ***phrases***. A phrase is a musical idea, like a sentence in a story. Most phrases in traditional music are four measures long. A phrase ends with a ***cadence***, which is a place of rest in music. A cadence is like the period at the end of a sentence. Cadences consist of two chords which bring a phrase to a close.

There are two types of cadences: ***final*** and ***non-final***. Final cadences bring a phrase to a complete ending. Non-final cadences look forward, and do not complete a musical idea. Another phrase is required to complete their non-final character.

Study Figure 9.1. Each line presents a pair of phrases. The phrases move in continuous quarter notes until they pause on a half-note. Harmonically, the most important chord in a phrase is the last one. This is the target or goal of the phrase. It acts in the same way that a comma, question mark or period acts in a sentence. This harmonic event at the end of a phrase is called a cadence.

Figure 9.1

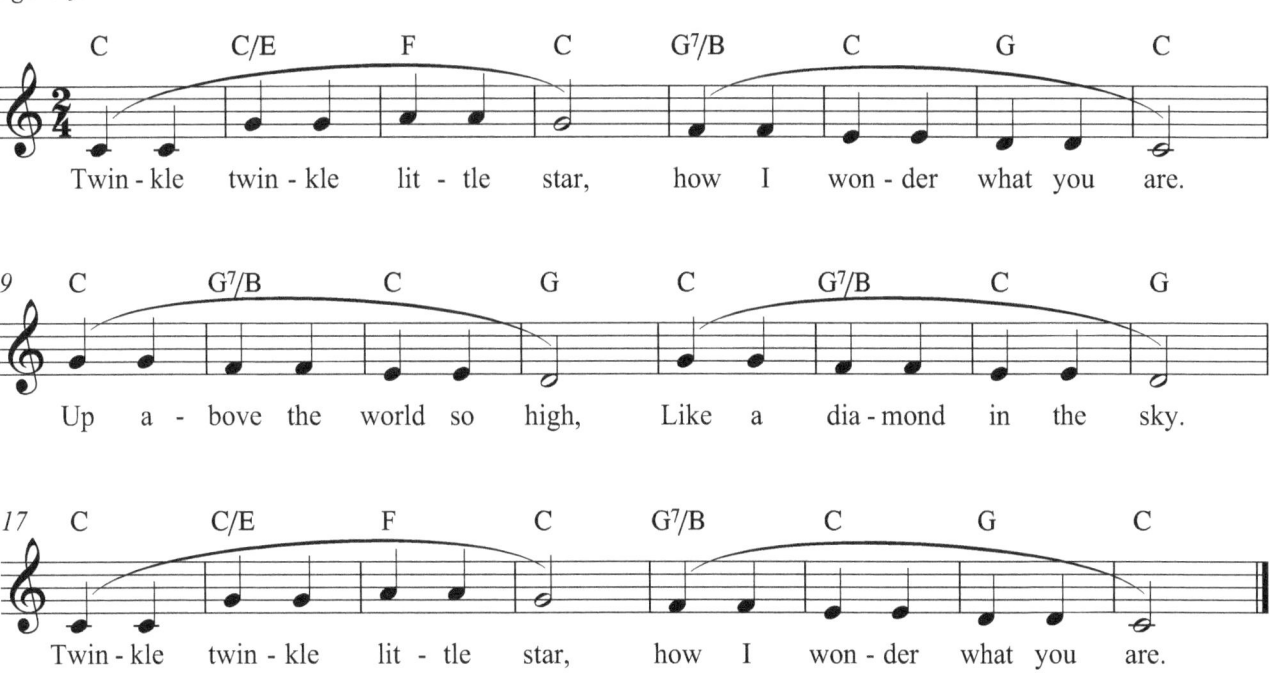

The Authentic Cadence

The most frequently used final cadence is the **authentic cadence**. It is the strongest and most conclusive cadence. It consists of the chords V - I or V - i (in minor keys). Figure 9.2 contains two authentic cadences in keyboard style. Notice the following common features of these cadences.

- They occur on the last two notes of the phrase.
- The first chord is on a weaker beat than the second chord.
- The V chord in a minor key contains raised $\hat{7}$.
- In keyboard style, three notes of the chord are placed in the treble staff, and the bass staff has the root of each chord.
- These cadences are considered *perfect authentic cadences* because they end with the tonic as the top note of the I chord. In the D major cadence, D is the final and top note. In the E minor cadence, E is the final and top note. Ending on the tonic confirms the key and gives the cadence a strong final sound.

Figure 9.2

The cadences in Figure 9.3 are considered *imperfect authentic cadences* because they end on a note other than the tonic in the upper part. The D major cadence ends with the 5th (A) as the final and top note. The E minor cadence ends with the 3rd (G) as the final and top note. These are still final cadences but do not sound as strong and final as a perfect authentic cadence which ends with the tonic as the top note.

Figure 9.3

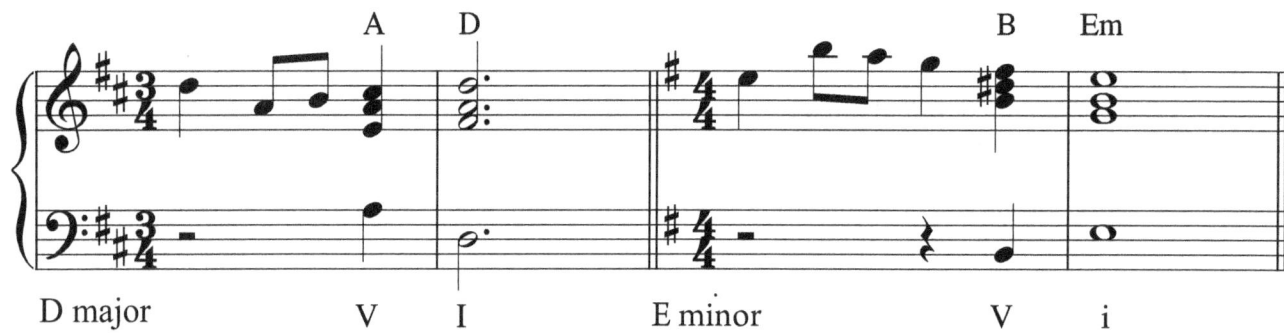

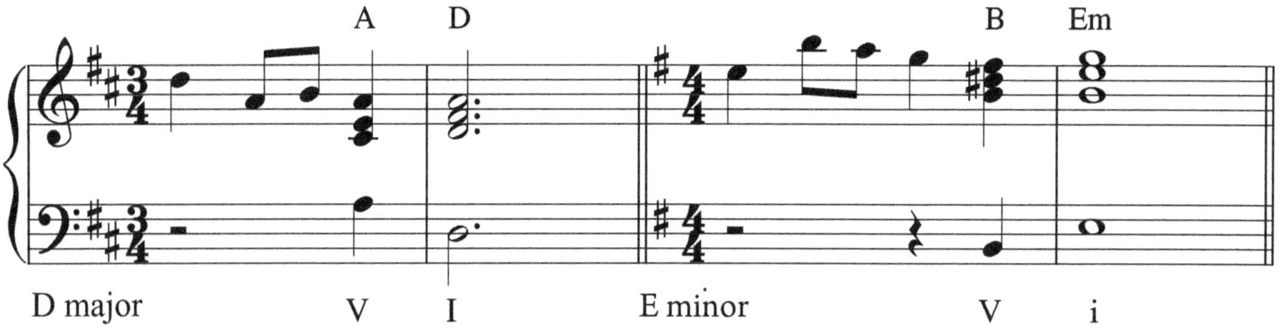

V^7 - I is also an authentic cadence. Figure 9.4 shows two authentic cadences using V^7. In the first example in G major, the V^7 chord is complete using all four notes, D F♯ A C. In the D minor example the V^7 chord is considered incomplete. Here, the root is doubled, and the 5th of the chord is left out, A C♯ G A. Both of these examples are correct. The root of each chord must be in the bass. The cadence in G major is a *perfect authentic cadence* and the cadence in D minor in an *imperfect authentic cadence*.

Figure 9.4

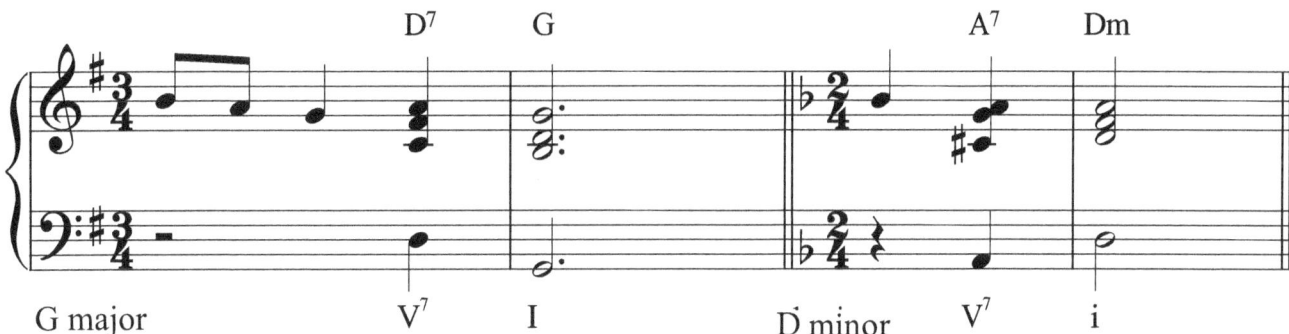

1. For the following authentic cadences: Name the key, write the functional and root/quality chord symbols and name them as perfect authentic or imperfect authentic.

key: _____

cadence: _____

key: _____

cadence: _____

key: _____

cadence: _____

key: _____

cadence: _____

Cadences

The Half Cadence

The *half cadence* is a non-final cadence. It ends on the V chord. Ending a phrase on the V chord leaves the music with an open or unfinished sound. For this reason, a piece of music does not end with a half cadence. Half cadences never end on the dominant seventh (V^7). V^7 contains too many strong tones that do not allow a feeling of rest. We will study two half cadences, I - V and IV - V.

Study the half cadences in keyboard style in Figure 9.5.

Figure 9.5

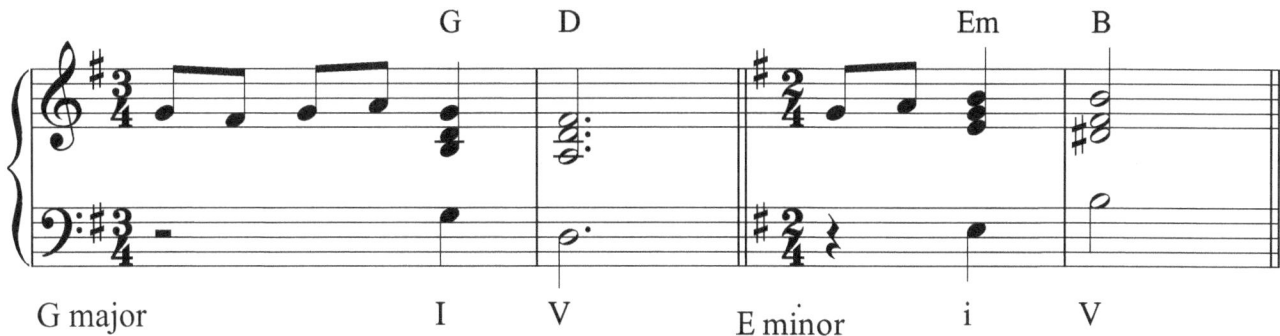

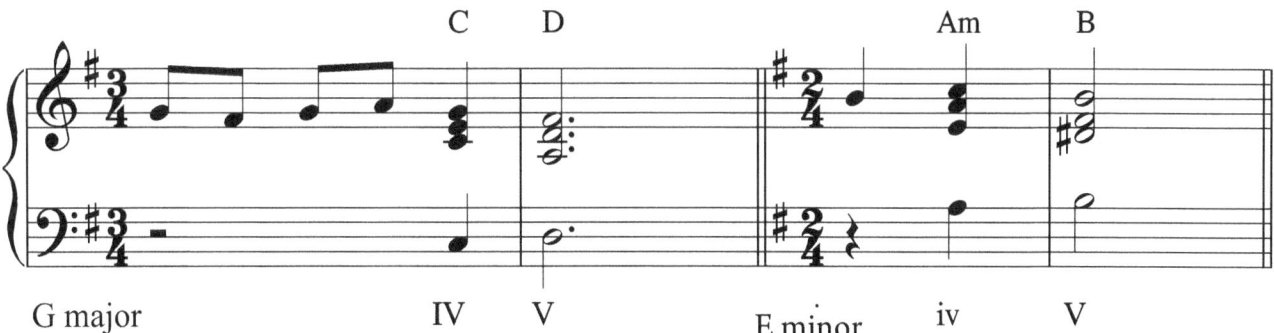

1. For the following cadences: Name the key, write the functional and root/quality chord symbols and name them as half, perfect authentic, or imperfect authentic.

10

Transposition

Music may be transposed from one key to another. Major key melodies can only be transposed to other major keys and minor keys to other minor keys.

Transposition Up By Interval

A melody can be transposed up by a specific interval. For example, you can transpose a melody up a perfect 5th, or a minor 3rd, or a major 2nd, or any other interval. Here are the steps for transposing a melody up by the interval of a major 3rd:

1. Determine the key of the original melody. You have to know what key you are starting in before you can determine the key to which you are going. The melody in Figure 10.1 is in F major.

Figure 10.1

Traditional
Early One Morning

2. Determine the interval of a major 3rd above F. Figure 10.2 shows that a major 3rd above F is A. The new key will be A major. The key signature of A major is three sharps. A major key can only be transposed to another major key.

Figure 10.2

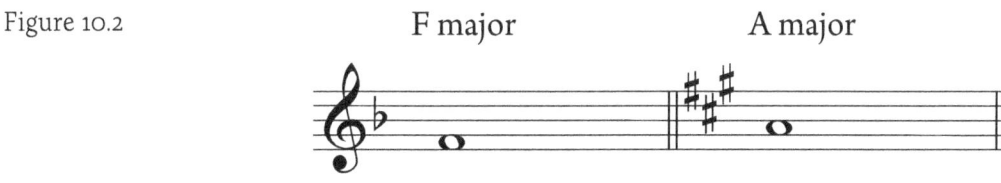

The interval of a major 3rd above F is A

3. Write the new key signature. In this case, three sharps for A major. Rewrite the melody moving every note up a 3rd. The key signature takes care of the quality of the intervals in the transposition. Copy everything from the original including the time signature, composer, dynamics, etc. Be sure to follow the normal rules of stem direction. Figure 10.3 contains the original melody transposed into the key of A major.

Figure 10.3

Traditional
Early One Morning

A major

You can only transpose from one major key to another major key. Even if you transpose by a minor interval, the melody still remains major. Figure 10.4 is in F major and contains two accidentals. Let's transpose it up a minor 3rd.

Figure 10.4

F major

A minor 3rd above F is A♭. The new key will be A♭ major. Write the key signature of A♭ major (4 flats), add the time signature, and move every note up a 3rd. There are 2 accidentals that will be part of the transposition. Beat 1 of m.2 is lowered one half step in the original and must be lowered in the transposed version. Beat 2 of m.3 is raised one half step in the original and must be raised in the transposed version.

Figure 10.5

A♭ major

Figure 10.6 is the original F major melody transposed up a minor 2nd to the key of G♭ major.

Figure 10.6

G♭ major

1. In the following examples you are given the original key. Transpose the tonic of these keys by the following intervals. Write the new key signature, the new tonic, and name the key.

2. Name the key of the following melody. Transpose it according to the given intervals. Name the new keys.

Traditional
Drink to Me Only

Key: _____

Transpose up a maj 3rd

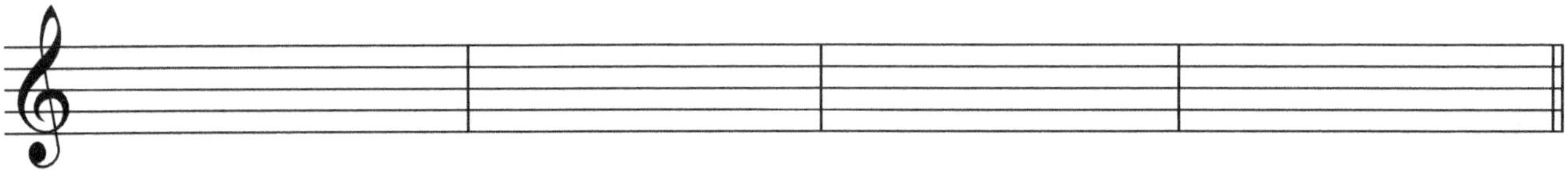

Key: _____

Transpose up a per 5th

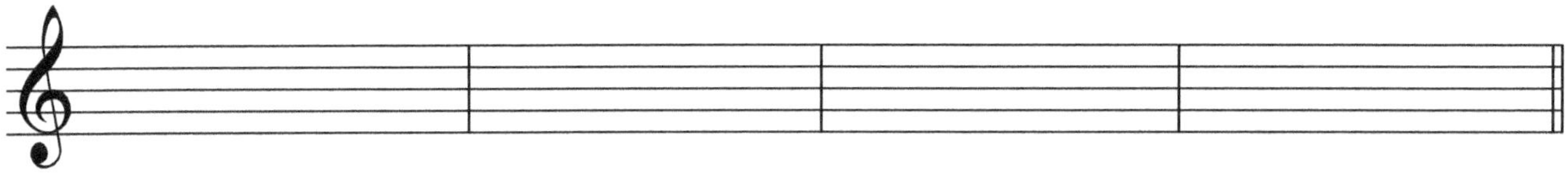

Key: _____

Transpose up a maj 6th

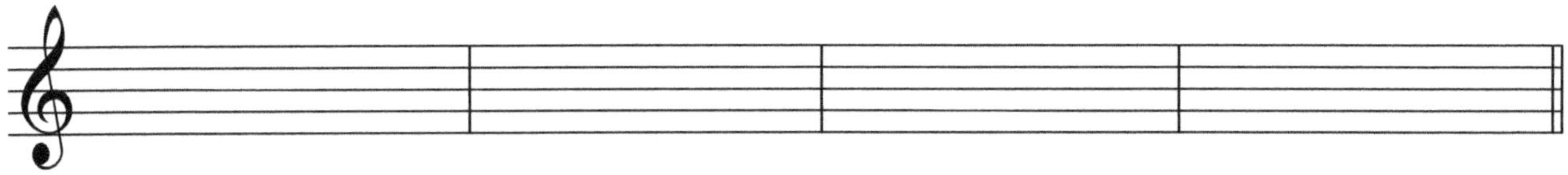

Key: _____

Transpose up a min 7th

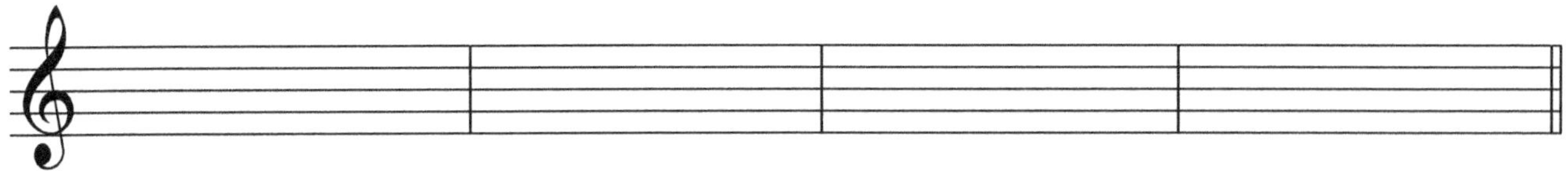

Key: _____

Transpostion By Key

You may be asked to transpose to a specific key. The steps for this are similar to transposing by interval. To transpose a melody into the key of B♭ major:

1. Determine the key of the original melody. The melody in Figure 10.7 is in G major.

Figure 10.7

G major

2. The distance from G to B♭ is up a minor 3rd. Write the key signature of B♭ major and move every note from the original melody up a 3rd. Copy everything from the original including the time signature, composer, tempo, etc. follow the rules of stem direction. Figure 10.8 contains the original melody transposed into the key of B♭ major.

Figure 10.8

B♭ major

1. Name the key of the following melody. Transpose it **up** to the indicated keys.

key: _____

D major

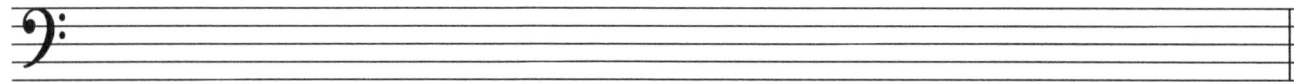

E♭ major

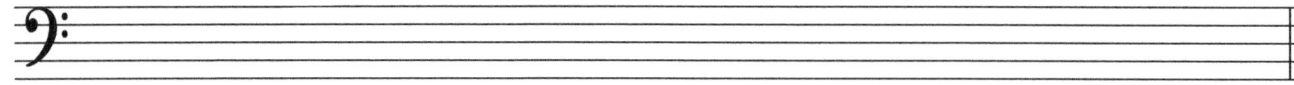

B major

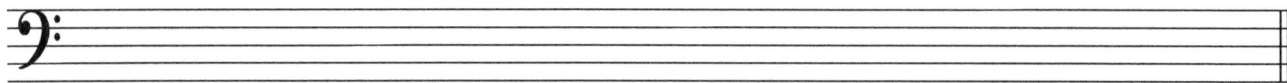

A major

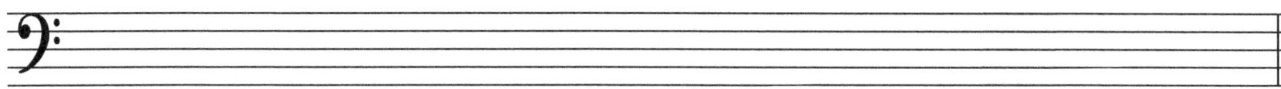

Transposition

11

Melody

Form and Melodic Structure

Music can be organized into sections. The overall organization of these sections is called *form*. The form of a composition shows its structure and can help the listener relate to, and understand what the composer is saying.

Once a composer chooses a form, they write musical ideas that eventually become the sections of a piece. These musical ideas are called ***phrases***, and they act as musical sentences that help make up the sections of a composition. Much like a paragraph, the sentences contribute meaning to the larger idea of the musical section. Visually, we can identify phrases by counting measures and looking for long notes or rests. Generally speaking, phrases are typically four measures long and end on a long note, like a half note, or on a rest. This acts like the period of a sentence, giving a slight pause between each phrase.

Composers don't usually throw together musical phrases in random order and hope that it works out. Instead, they can plan to have a question and answer type of phrasing structure, where the phrases work in pairs to construct a section of music. This section is called a ***period***. A period is usually eight measures long consisting of two four measure phrases.

The first phrase, or 'question,' is called the ***antecedent phrase***. This makes sense because the prefix 'ante' means 'before' or 'preceding.' The antecedent phrase usually ends on a note that makes it feel unfinished or makes the listener want more. This could be an unstable scale degree like $\hat{2}$ or $\hat{7}$, leading to a non-final cadence. Half cadences are non-final and leave the music with an open or unfinished sound.

The resolution happens in the second phrase, the 'answer,' which is called the **consequent phrase**. The prefix 'con' means 'with.' This makes sense because the suffix 'sequence' means a 'series' or one thing following another. This phrase usually ends on a stable scale degree like $\hat{1}$ and supports a final cadence.

Study the melody in Figure 11.1. The end of the first phrase feels like the melody is not quite done because it ends on the unstable scale degree $\hat{2}$. The phrase is four measures long and ends on a half note, giving pause before the next phrase begins.

The second phase in Figure 11.1 is very similar to the first phrase. The difference between the two phrases is the ending. The second phrase ends on a stable pitch $(\hat{1})$. Since the second phrase uses the same melody as the first with a slight variation, the two phrases are labeled **a** and **a¹**. This type of melody construction, with two similar phrases, is called a **parallel period**.

Figure 11.1

G major

Implied Harmony

The notes of a melody can imply or suggest certain chords that could go along with it. This is called the ***implied harmony***. Figure 11.2 contains the I, IV, and V chords in G major.

Figure 11.2

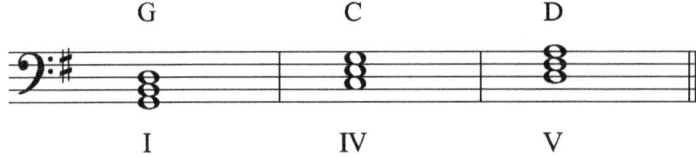

Chords can be used with a melody if they contain the same notes as those found in the melody. The implied harmony for our original melody is suggested in Figure 11.3.

The G and the B in m.1 suggest chord I in G major. It is the opening measure. Most pieces begin with the tonic chord. This helps to establish the key or tonality. The eighth note A in m.1 is not part of the G chord (GBD). This note provides movement to the melody and connects the two chord tones G and B. It is called a ***passing tone***. Passing tones are called ***non-chord tones***. These are notes that are not part of the underlying chord.

The two C's in m.2 imply the IV chord (CEG) in G major.

The D and G in m.3 imply the I chord, and the A in m.4 implies the V chord.
It is important that the notes at the end of a melodic phrase imply a logical cadence.
Here I - V implies a half cadence. The end of a phrase must have a logical cadence.

The D and the F♯ in m.7 imply V (DF♯A), and the final note in m.8, G, implies I. This implies a perfect authentic cadence in G major.

Ending a phrase on the tonic and approaching it from a step below ($\hat{7}$ - $\hat{1}$) or from a step above ($\hat{2}$ - $\hat{1}$) is extremely strong melodically and tonally. It suggests a perfect authentic cadence and effectively reinforces the key.

Figure 11.3

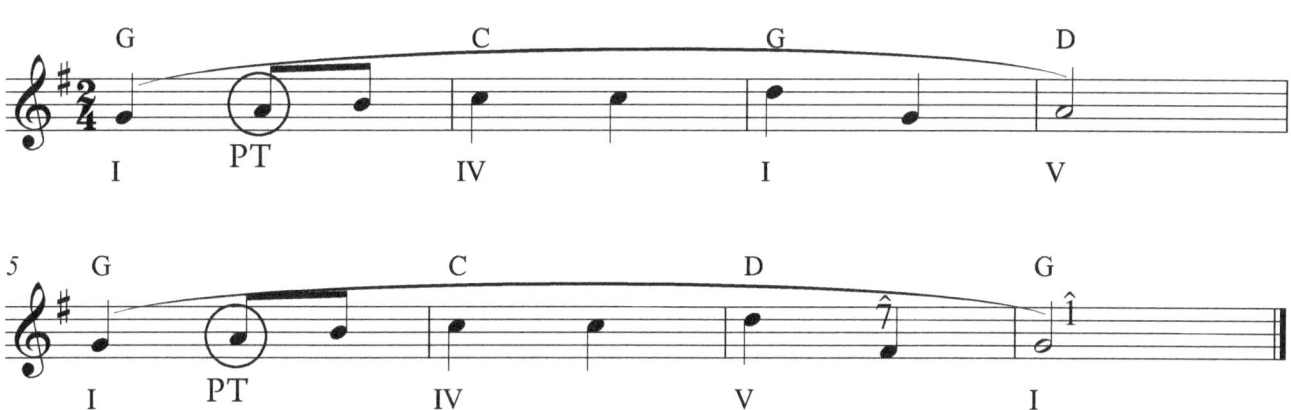

1. Name the key of each of the following parallel periods. Using Roman numerals I, IV, and V, write the implied harmony under each. Circle and mark any passing tones PT.

key:_____

key:_____

key:_____

Melody

Writing a Melody

At this level we are going to write a two phrase melody based on two given measures.

Figure 11.4 contains two measures of a melody. Study the steps for writing a two phrase melody based on these measures.

Figure 11.4

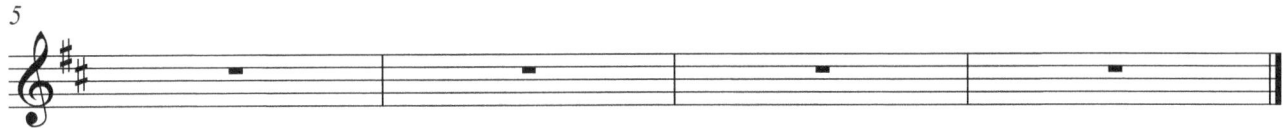

1. Name the key. This melody is in D major.

2. Make a structural plan and label the sections "a" and "a¹" to show the question and answer phrases.

3. Decide on the implied harmony for the existing measures.

4. Sketch in the implied harmony for the remaining measures. In this example, I and V are used for mm.3 and 4, implying a half cadence at the end of the first phrase. Since this is a parallel period, the second phrase (a¹) begins with a repeat of mm.1 and 2. The implied harmony for mm.7 and 8 is V - I suggesting an authentic cadence.

5. Add the root/quality chord symbols above the staff.

6. Complete the opening measures of "a¹" by copying mm.1 and 2 into mm. 5 and 6.

6. Complete the first phrase by writing the melody in mm. 3 and 4. This phrase should end on an unstable degree like $\hat{2}$ or $\hat{7}$. Here, it ends on $\hat{2}$. This supports a half cadence which is ideal for the question portion of this melody.

7. This two measure response uses similar rhythmic values to those found in the opening measures. Try to stick to a similar rhythm to maintain rhythmic unity in your writing. The use of an unrelated rhythm may not make sense or seem out of place.

8. The first phrase ends on a dotted half note. This works well since a cadence is a place of rest and requires a slowing of the rhythm. The cadence occurs over the bar with I on a weak beat and V on a strong beat. This is the typical rhythm of a cadence. The second chord of a cadence usually ends on a stronger beat than the first chord.

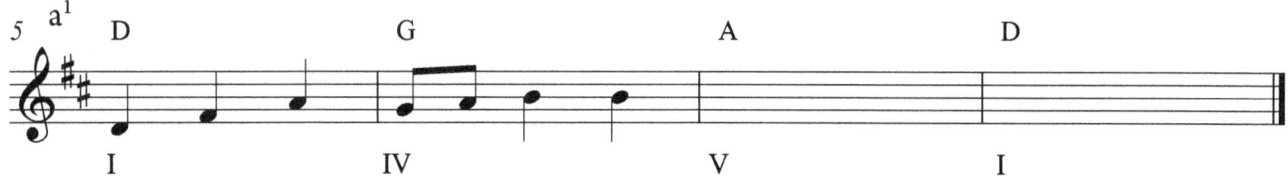

9. Complete the final two measures of the second phrase. This phrase should end on a stable chord tone. Here, it ends on $\hat{1}$ and is approached by $\hat{7}$. Concluding a phrase with $\hat{7}$ - $\hat{1}$ or $\hat{2}$ - $\hat{1}$ in the melody is extremely strong and supports a perfect authentic cadence.

10. The rhythm of the final two measures matches the rhythm of mm. 3 and 4. Although this is not necessary, it provides rhythmic unity.

11. Indicate each phrase by adding phrase marks.

1. For the following melodic fragments:

    i. Name the key.
    ii. Label the formal structure using "a" and "a¹."
    iii. Complete the first phrase according to the given implied harmony.
    iv. If not already given, indicate the implied harmony for the second phrase.
    v. Write the second phrase creating a *parallel period*.
    vi. Add root/quality chord symbols to both phrases.
    vii. Mark each phrase.

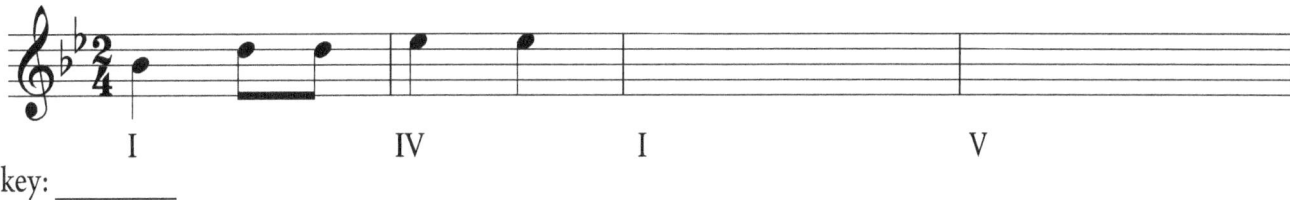

key: _____

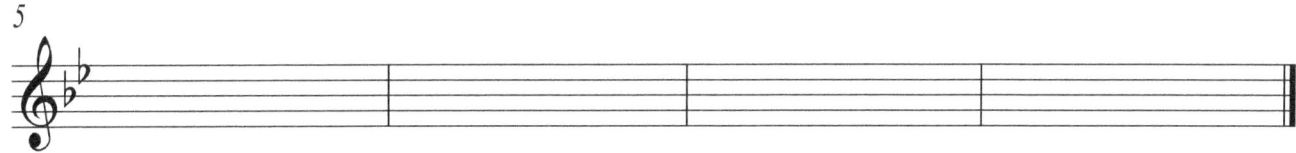

key: _____

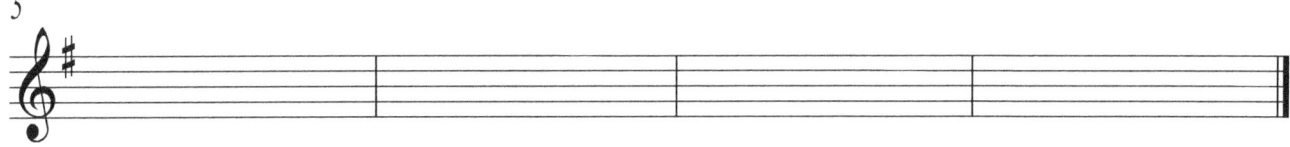

key: _____

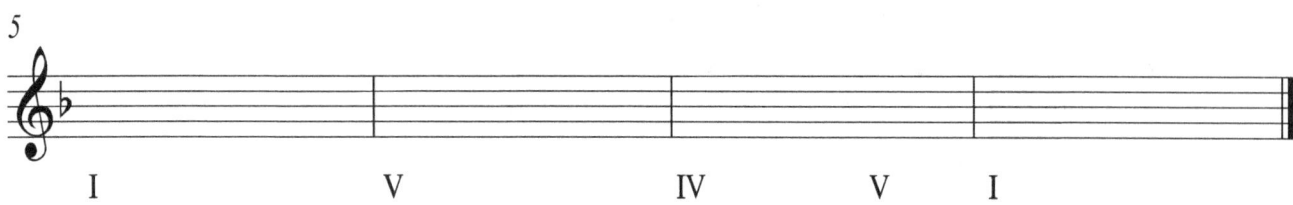

key: _____

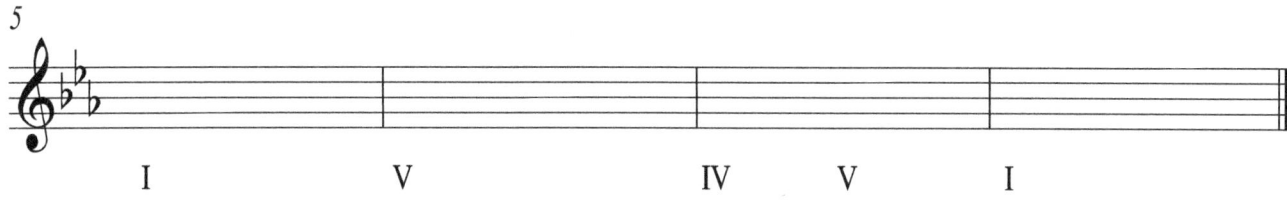

key: _____

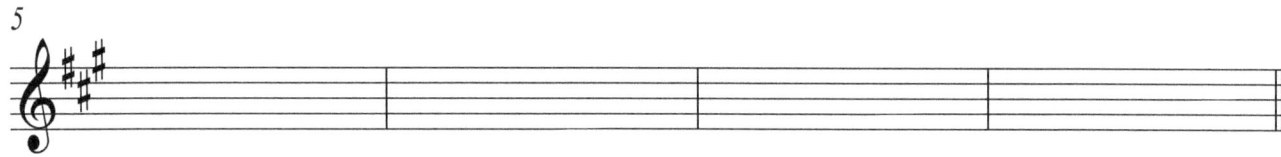

12
History 3

The Classical Era (ca 1750 - 1825)

The Classical era follows the Baroque era. Music from the Classical era was composed around 1750 to 1825.

Classical music is clear, structured and balanced. Form is very important, as well as harmony and tonality—that is, the key in which a piece is written.

Classical music uses dynamic contrast to emphasize movement from the tonic to new keys and then a return to the tonic. It is often loud one moment and then soft the next. It changes volume frequently. It is different from Baroque music in that it is simpler in style, without the heavy figurations and ornamentation. It is not polyphonic, that is, there is no weaving together of different tunes like those found in Baroque music.

Classical music often has a clear tune or melody with an accompaniment. Music with a single line of melody and a harmonic accompaniment is called **homophonic music** or **homophony**.

Most classical music is **absolute music**. This means that it is written specifically for the sake of being music. There are no pictorial or literary associations. It is not supposed to depict or portray anything. It's just beautiful music!

Large forms featured in the Classical period include the solo sonata, symphony, and the concerto. This period also saw a rise in **chamber music**. Chamber music is composed for smaller groups of musicians. These groups consist of two to ten players, with one player on each part. Examples of chamber music include trios, quartets, and quintets.

The greatest composers of the classical period are:

Joseph Haydn (1732–1809).
Wolfgang Amadeus Mozart (1756–1791).
Ludwig van Beethoven (1770–1827).

The classical period ended before Beethoven died. In fact, Beethoven was the one who ended it. Beethoven's later music was so new and unique that it had to be called something completely different.

Sonata Form in the Classical Era

Sonata form reached its zenith in the Classical era at the hands of Haydn, Mozart, and Beethoven.

Sonata form consists of three main sections:

1. **The exposition**: this is the opening section of sonata form. In this section, the composer introduces themes or melodies. Often there are two contrasting themes in two contrasting keys. Contrasting key or tonality is an essential part of this form.
2. **The development**: this is the middle section, and the composer *develops* the themes stated in the exposition. This developing is often done through movement to different keys.
3. **The recapitulation**: in this section the composer returns to the main themes stated in the exposition. This section does not usually change key and remains in the tonic throughout.

Sonata form was used as the basis for movements of solo sonatas, symphonies, concertos and chamber music.

Eine Kleine Nachtmusik (1st Mvt.) Wolfgang Amadeus Mozart

Wolfgang Amadeus Mozart (1756 - 1791) was one of the most important composers of the Classical era. He composed over 600 works, including some of the worlds most famous symphonies, chamber music, operas, and choral music.

Mozart gave the name **Eine kleine Nachtmusik** to his Serenade No. 13 for strings in G major, K 525. It is one of his most popular pieces, and the opening theme is famous. It was composed in 1787.

The title Eine kleine Nachtmusik means: "A little Night Music." "Nachtmusik" was a title that was given to serenades in the 18th century.

The genre of this work is chamber music. It is composed for two violins, viola, and cello and optional double bass. It can be performed as a string quartet or by a small group of string instruments, with one added double bass.

The first movement of Eine kleine Nachtmusik is in sonata form.

The complete work consists of 4 movements.

Music Terms

Study the following music terms

secondo, seconda	second, lower part of a duet
sempre	always
senza	without
sforzando, sf, sfz	sudden strong accent on a single note or chord
simile	continue in the same manner as has been indicated
subito	suddenly
tre corde	three strings, release the left pedal on the piano
troppo	too much
una corda	one string, depress the left pedal on the piano

Review 3

1. For the following melodies: Name the key. At the end of each phrase write the functional and root/quality chord symbols and name each cadence as half, perfect authentic, or imperfect authentic.

key: _____

cadence: _____

cadence: _____

key: _____

cadence: _____

cadence: _____

2. Name the key of the following melody. Transpose it according to the instructions.

Gustav Holst
Hymn Tune

key: ___________

Up a minor 3rd

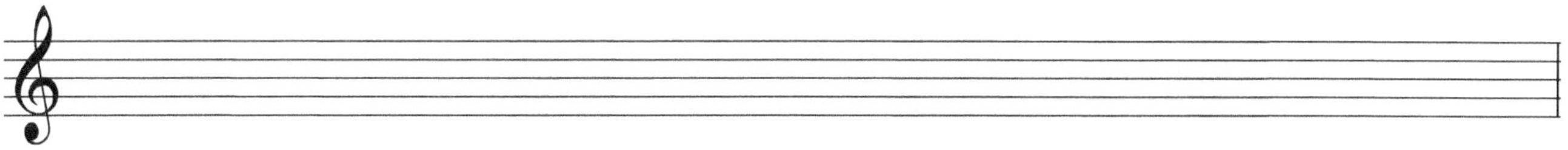

key: ___________

Up to A major

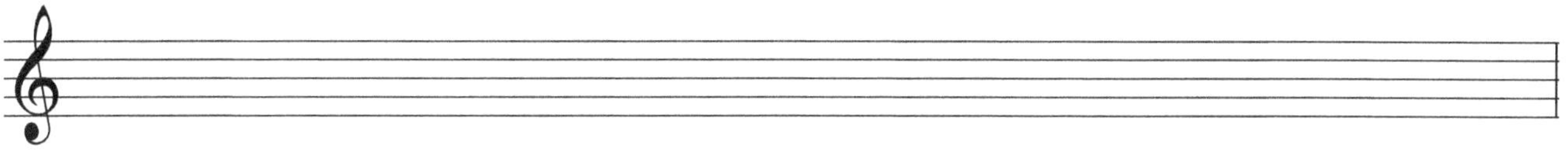

Name the interval of transposition: __________

3. For the following melodic fragment: Name the key. Complete the first phrase according to the given chord symbols. End this phrase on an unstable scale degree. Write an answer phrase creating a parallel period and ending on a stable degree. Mark the phrasing.

key: ___________

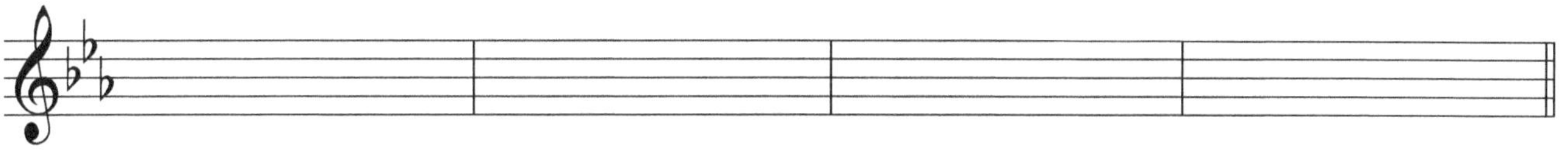

4. Match the Italian term with its definition.

1. *una corda*   _____second, lower part of a duet

2. *tre corde*   _____always

3. *subito*   _____without

4. *troppo*   _____sudden strong accent on a single note or chord

5. *simile*   _____continue in the same manner as has been indicated

6. *senza*   _____suddenly

7. *sempre*   _____three strings, release the left pedal on the piano

8. *sforzando, sf, sfz*   _____too much

9. *secondo, seconda*   _____one string, depress the left pedal on the piano

5. Answer the following questions as true (T) or false (F).

a. The classical period occured around 1750 to 1825. _____
b. The 3 major composers of the classical period are Haydn, Mozart and Bach. _____
c. Music with a single melodic line and accompaniment is *homophonic*. _____
d. Most classical music is *program music*. _____
e. Sonata form consists of 3 main sections. _____
f. These sections are: the *exhibition*, the *development* and the *recapitulation*. _____
g. Eine kleine Nachtmusik is *chamber music*. _____
h. Eine kleine Nachtmusisk is written for strings. _____
i. Eine kleine Nachtmusik contains 5 movements. _____
j. The first movement of Eine kleine Nachtmusik is in *sonata form*. _____

13

Music Analysis

Form - Review

One of the basic units of organization in a composition is the *phrase*. A composer may use groups of phrases to form sections, and the sections may be put together to create specific forms. Like the sentences in a story that work together to create a paragraph, phrases are musical sentences that work together to create a section.

Composers often write pairs of phrases that have a question and answer structure and work together to create a section of music. These are called *antecedent* (question) and *consequent* (answer) phrases.

The two phrases in Figure 13.1 create a section called a *parallel period*. The first phrase (*a*) ends on an unstable scale degree implying a half cadence. The second phrase (*a¹*) repeats much of the melodic material from the first phrase but ends on a stable scale degree implying an authentic cadence. Because the two phrases are very similar melodically, they are given the labels *a* and *a¹*.

Figure 13.1

The two phrases in Figure 13.2 create a section called a contrasting period. In a contrasting period, the melodic material is different (or contrasting) between the two phrases. The first phrase (*a*) ends on an unstable scale degree implying a half cadence. The second phrase uses different melodic material than the first phrase and is given the label *b*. It ends on a stable pitch implying an authentic cadence.

Figure 13.2

Binary Form

Sections similar to those found in Figure 13.1 and 13.2 can be combined to create larger musical forms. One of the most simple forms is **binary form**. The prefix 'bi" means 'two.' A piece in binary form consists of two different or contrasting sections that are labelled **A** and **B**. Lowercase letters are used to label the single phrases of the parallel and contrasting period. Uppercase letters are used to label the sections in binary form because they are larger.

Figure 13.3 contains the folk song *Greensleeves*. This is an example of a 16 measure piece in binary form. It consists of two parallel periods. The first 8 measure section is given the label **A**. The second 8 measure section is contrasting to the A section, and given the label **B**. The phrases of the A section could be labelled *a* and *a¹* and the phrases of the B section could be labelled *b* and *b¹*. However, when analyzing binary form, the phrases are not always so cut and dry. Binary form is just labelled with A and B to reflect the two larger contrasting sections.

Figure 10.3

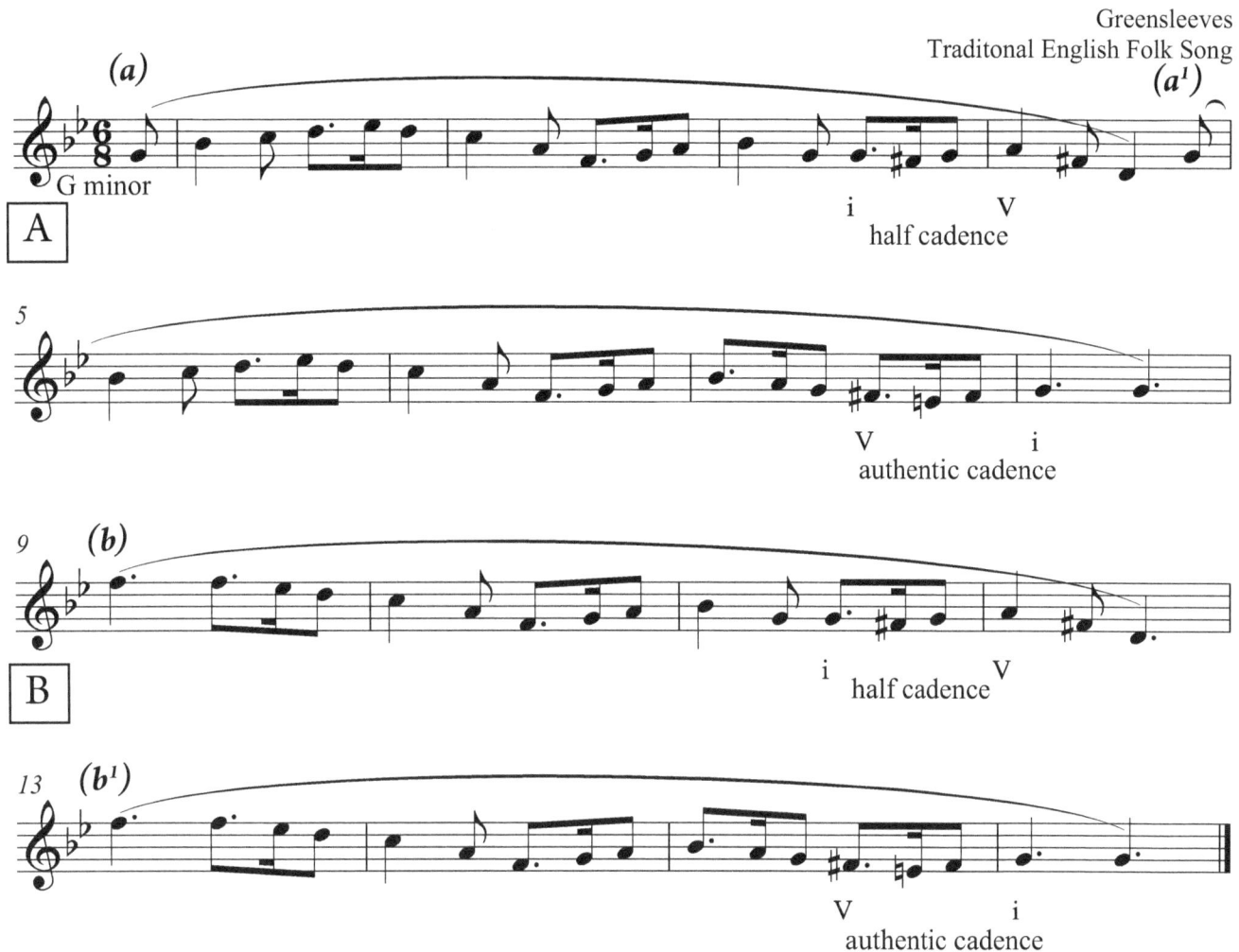

Ternary Form

Study Figure 13.4. This piece is in a three-part form called **ternary form** (ABA). The prefix 'ter' means 'three.' This form has three parts labelled A - B - A. In ternary form, the A section always returns after a contrasting B section.

In Figure 13.4 the first section (mm.1 - 8) is labelled A. The second contrasting section (mm. 9 - 16)is labelled B. The final section (mm. 17 - 24) is an exact repetition of the first section, and is labelled A. Sometimes the final A section is not an exact repitition of the first section. The composer may shorten, lengthen, alter the melody slightly, or vary the accompaniment of the final A section. In this case the form would be analyzed as ABA[1] to reflect this variation.

Figure 13.4

Wolfgang Amadeus Mozart
12 Variations on "Ah vous dirai-je Maman"

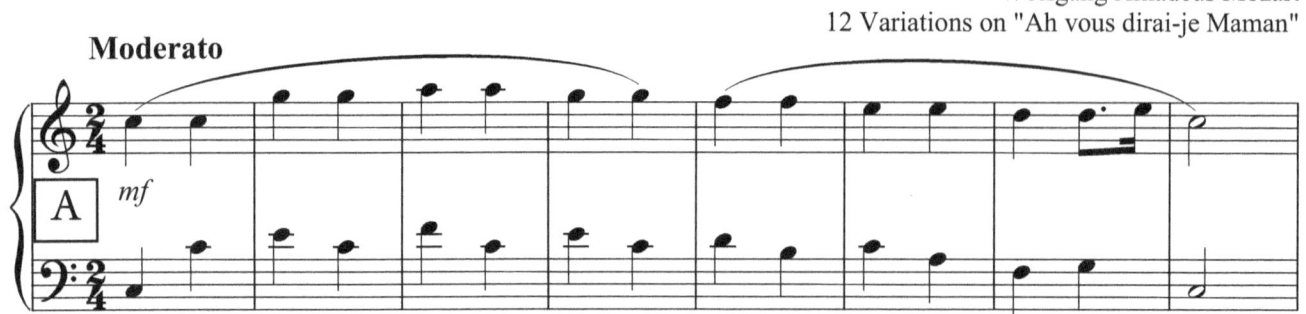

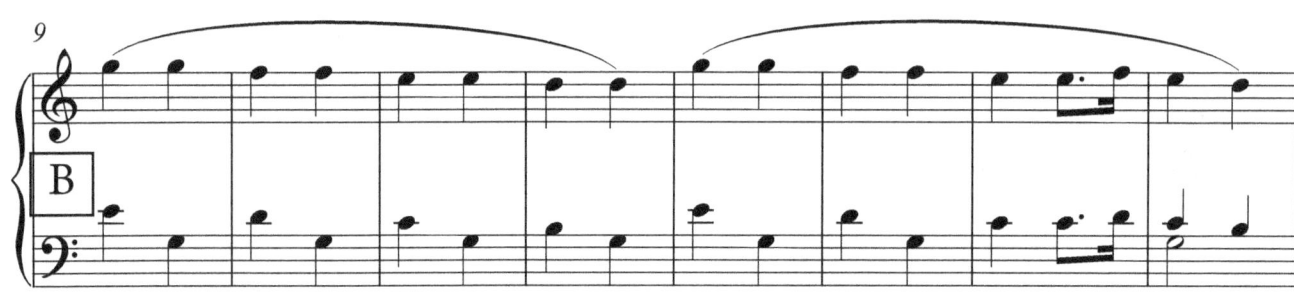

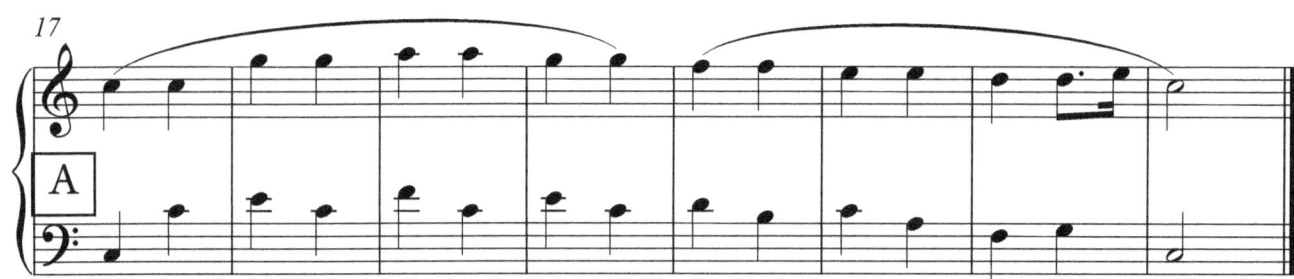

Binary and ternary forms are fairly simple, but they act as a basis for more complex forms in classical music. Phrases are used to organize a piece. Antecedent and consequent phrases are grouped to form periods. The periods come together to make sections, and the sections come together to make a composition. The sections vary by musical idea and are identified and labeled by their contrast or difference from one another. Compositions with the AB structure are in binary form, and compositions with ABA or ABA[1] are in ternary form.

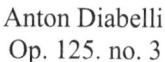

Anton Diabelli
Op. 125. no. 3

1. Name the key of this piece. _____

2. Write the time signature directly on the score.

3. The form of this piece is: ❑binary   ❑ternary

4. Label the score by using A, A¹, and B to define the form.

5. Define *Allegretto*. _____

6. Check all statements below that apply to the chord at A:

   ❑tonic triad   ❑subdominant triad   ❑C major triad   ❑root position   ❑broken chord

7. Check all statements below that apply to the chord at B:

   ❑tonic triad   ❑dominant triad   ❑G major triad   ❑1st inversion   ❑solid or blocked chord

8. Name the cadence at C:

   ❑perfect authentic cadence   ❑half cadence   ❑imperfect authentic cadence

9. Symbolize the chords of this cadence on the score using functional chord symbols.

Anton Diabelli
Op. 125 No. 4

Moderato

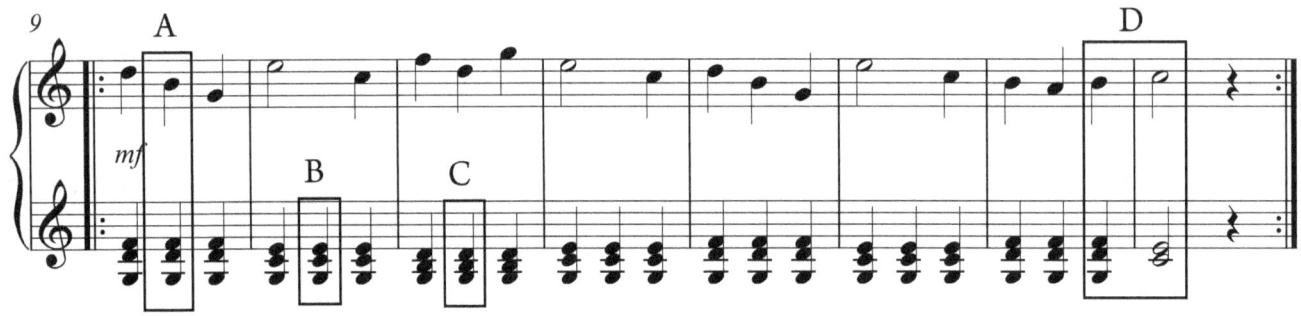

1. Name the key of this piece. _____

2. Write the time signature directly on the score.

3. Check the words below that apply to this time signature.

    ❑triple   ❑compound   ❑duple   ❑simple   ❑quadruple

4. Mark the phrases using a slur.

5. The form of this piece is: ❑binary   ❑ternary

6. Label the score by using A, A¹, and B to define the form.

7. Define **Moderato**. _____

8. Name the chord at letter A: _____

9. For the chord at letter B name the: root_____ quality_____ position_____

10. For the chord at letter C name the: root_____ quality_____ position_____

11. The cadence at D is: ❑half   ❑perfect authentic   ❑imperfect authentic

12. Write the functional chord symbols for this cadence directly on the score.

13. Find and circle a broken dominant triad on the score. Label it DT.

14. Find and circle a broken tonic triad on the score. Label it TT.

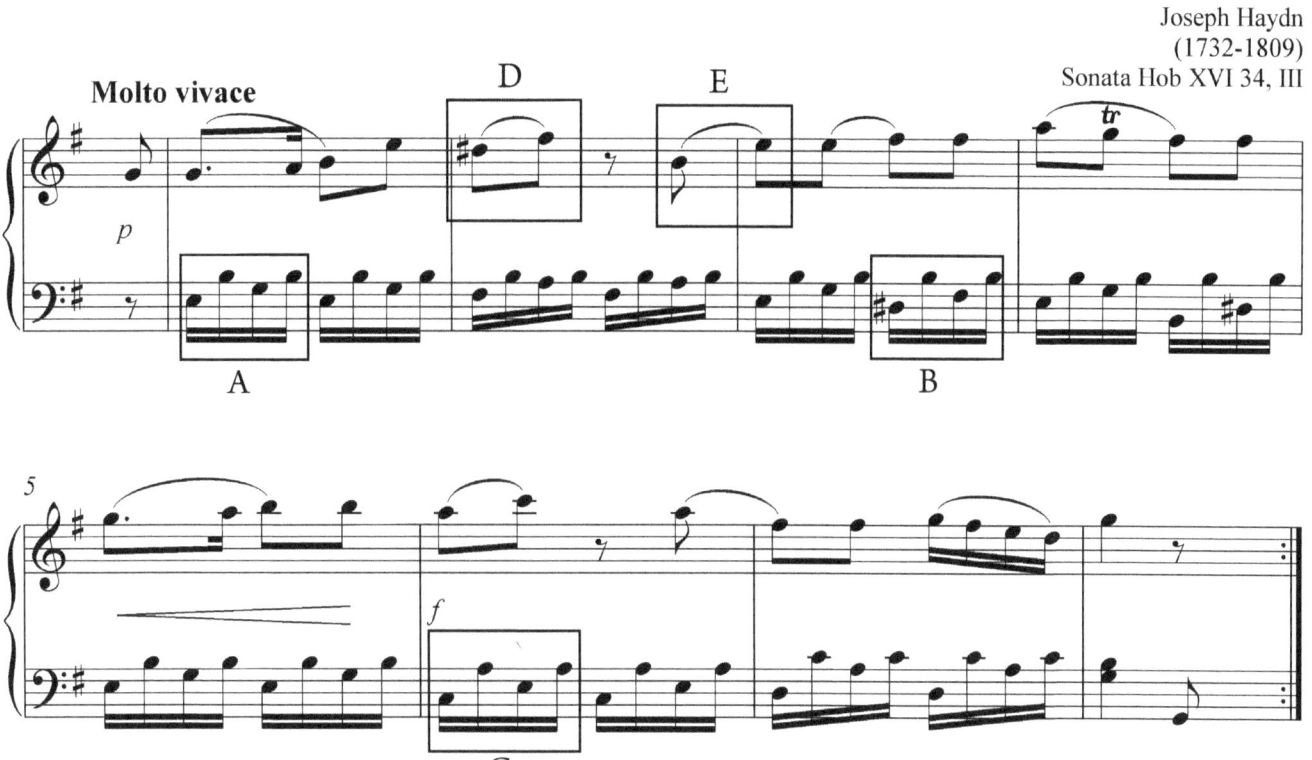

1. Name the key of this piece. _____
2. Write the time signature directly on the score.
3. This excerpt is written for a right hand melody with left hand accompaniment. This is and example of:
   ❏ polyphonic music   ❏ homophonic music   ❏ contrapuntal music   ❏ absolute music
4. What musical era was this piece composed? _____
5. Name the chord at A: root_____   quality_____   position_____
6. Name the chord at B: root_____   quality_____   position_____
7. Name the chord at C: root_____   quality_____   position_____
8. In this piece, chord A is the: ❏ tonic triad   ❏ subdominant triad   ❏ dominant triad
9. In this piece, chord B is the: ❏ tonic triad   ❏ subdominant triad   ❏ dominant triad
10. In this piece, chord C is the: ❏ tonic triad   ❏ subdominant triad   ❏ dominant triad
11. Define *Molto vivace*: _____
12. This excerpt is an example of a: ❏ parallel period   ❏ contrasting period
13. Name the interval at D: _____
14. Name the interval at E: _____

Music Terms and Signs

Terms

accelerando, accel.	becoming quicker
accent	a stressed note
ad libitum, ad lib.	at the liberty of the performer
adagio	slow
alla, all'	in the manner of
allegretto	fairly fast, a little slower than allegro
allegro	fast
andante	moderately slow, at a walking pace
andantino	a little faster than andante
animato	lively, animated
a tempo	return to the original tempo
ben, bene	well
cantabile	in a singing style
col, coll', colla, colle	with
con	with
con brio	with vigor
con espressione	with expression
con fuoco	with fire
con grazia	with grace
con moto	with motion
crescendo, cresc.	becoming louder
da capo, D.C.	from the beginning
D.C. al fine	repeat from the beginning and end at *Fine*
dal segno, D.S. 𝄋	from the sign
decrescendo, decresc.	becoming softer
diminuendo, dim.	becoming softer
dolce	sweetly, gentle
e, ed	and
espressivio, espress.	expressive, with expression

fine	the end
forte, f	loud
fortissimo, ff	very loud
fortepiano, fp	loud, then suddenly soft
grazioso	gracefully
grave	slow and solemn
larghetto	fairly slow, not as slow as largo
largo	very slow
leggiero	light
lento	slow
loco	return to the normal register
ma	but
maestoso	majestically
mano destra, m.d.	right hand
mano sinistra, m.s.	left hand
marcato	play marked or stressed
meno	less
meno mosso	less motion
mezzo forte, mf	moderately loud
mezzo piano, mp	moderately soft
moderato	at a moderate tempo
molto	much, very
non	not
ottava, 8va	the interval of an octave
pedale, ped	pedal
pianissimo, pp	very soft
piano, p	soft
piu	more
piu mosso	more motion
poco	little
poco a poco	little by little
prestissimo	as fast as possible

presto	very fast
primo, prima	first, the upper part of a duet
quasi	almost, as if
rallentando, rall.	slowing down
ritardando, rit.	slowing down gradually
rubato	flexible tempo with slight variations of speed to enhance musical expression.
secondo, seconda	second, lower part of a duet
sempre	always
senza	without
sforzando, sf, sfz	sudden strong accent on a single note or chord
simile	continue in the same manner as has just been indicated
staccato	play short and detached
subito	suddenly
tempo	speed at which music is performed
Tempo Primo, Tempo I	return to the original tempo
tranquillo	tranquil, quiet
tre corde	3 strings, release the left pedal on the piano
troppo	too much
una corda	1 string, depress the left pedal on the piano
vivace	lively, brisk

Signs

accent - a stressed note

common time - symbol for 4/4

crescendo - becoming louder

decrescendo - becoming softer

double bar line - the end of a piece

fermata - hold note or rest longer than written value

slur - play the notes smoothly (legato)

staccato - play short and detached

tie - hold for the combined value of the tied notes

repeat marks - at the second sign go back to the first sign and repeat the music from there. The first sign is left out if the music is repeated from the beginning.

tenuto mark - when placed over or under a note, hold it for its full value.

pedal symbol - press/release the right pedal.

dal segno, D.S. - from the sign.

   **8va** - play one octave higher than written pitch.

   **8va** - play one octave lower than written pitch.

          down bow - on a string instrument, play the note by drawing the bow downward.

          up bow - on a string instrument, play the note by drawing the bow upward.

          breath mark - take a breath or a small break

History Terms

Baroque era - ca. 1600 - 1750

polyphony: two or more melodies combined. Also known as **counterpoint**.

Invention: a polyphonic keyboard composition.

motives: short melodic and rhythmic ideas used to create a melody.

imitation: the technique of repeating a musical idea (motive) in another voice or part.

sequence: the repetition of a motive or phrase at a higher or lower pitch.

concerto grosso: a baroque work for orchestra. It usually has 3 movements and contains a group of solo instruments called the ***concertino*** that contrasts with the full string orchestra which is known as the ***ripieno***.

ritornello form: in this form, a repeated section of music, known as the ritornello alternates with different musical sections.

Classical era - ca. 1750 - 1825

homophonic music or *homophony*: music with a single line of melody and a harmonic accompaniment

absolute music: music that it is written specifically for the sake of music. There are no pictorial or literary associations. It is not supposed to depict or portray anything.

chamber music: music composed for smaller groups of musicians. These groups consist of two to ten players, with one player on each part. Examples of chamber music include trios, quartets, and quintets.

sonata form: a three part form consisting of the following sections:

1. **The exposition**: this is the opening section of sonata form. In this section the composer introduces themes or melodies. Most often there are 2 contrasting themes in 2 contrasting keys. Contrasting key or tonality is an essential part of this form.
2. **The development**: this is the middle section and the composer *develops* the themes stated in the exposition. This developing is often done through movement to different keys.
3. **The recapitulation**: in this section the composer returns to the main themes stated in the exposition. This section does not usually change key and remains in the tonic throughout.

Exam

(5) 1. Name the following intervals.

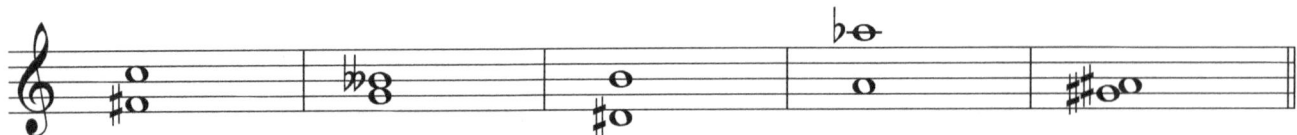

_____   _____   _____   _____   _____

(5) 2. Write the following intervals above the given notes.

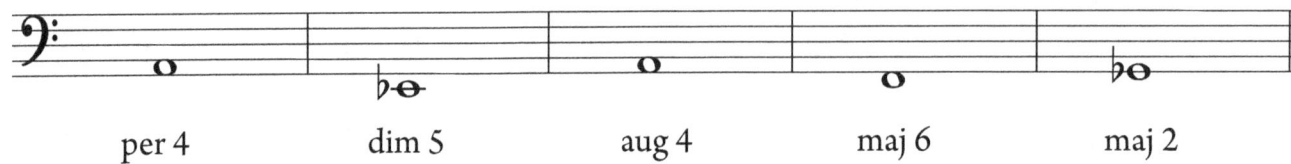

per 4   dim 5   aug 4   maj 6   maj 2

(5) 3. Name the key of the following melody. Write the root/quality and functional chord symbols implied by the melody.

key: _____

(10) 4. For the following melodic fragment: Name the key. Complete the first phrase according to the given chord symbols. End this phrase on an unstable scale degree. Write an answer phrase creating a parallel period and ending on a stable degree. Mark the phrasing.

key: _____

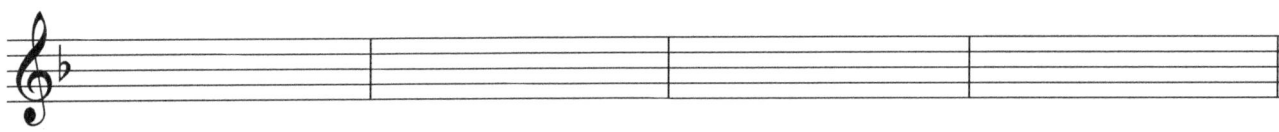

©San Marco Publications 2022

(10) 5. Complete the following measures with rests under the brackets.

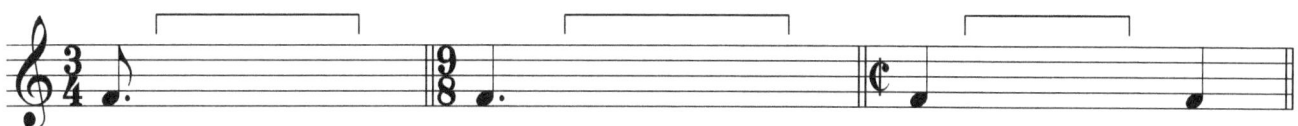

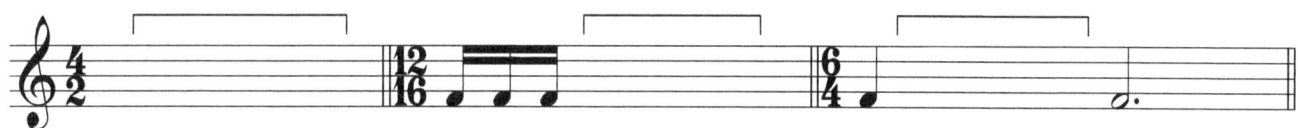

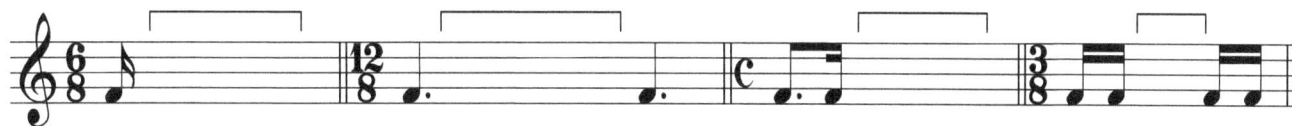

(10) 6. Name the key of the following melody. Add the time signature at the beginning of the score.

Muzio Clementi
Sonata for 4 Hands

Key: _____

Transpose it up an augmented 4th using a key signature. Name the key.

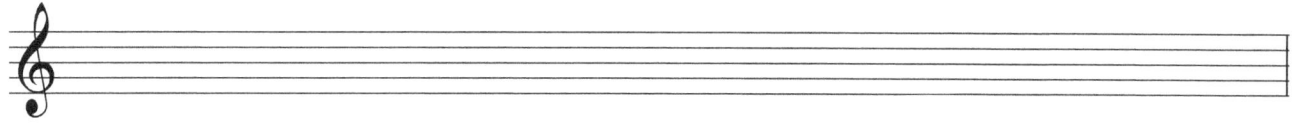

Key: _____

Transpose it **up** into the key of G major. Name the interval of transposition.

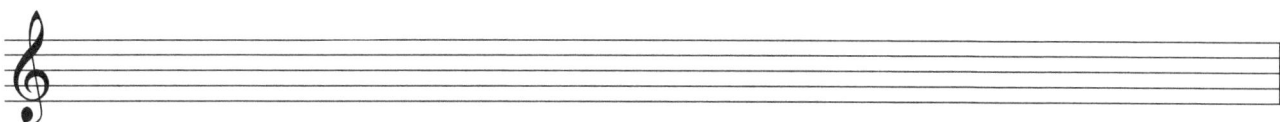

Interval of transposition: _____

©San Marco Publications 2022

7. Write the following chords using key signatures for each.

　i.　the mediant triad of E major in root position
　ii.　the leading tone triad of D harmonic minor, first inversion
　iii.　the subdominant triad of D flat major in root position
　iv.　the dominant 7th chord in A flat major in root position
　v.　the tonic triad of C sharp natural minor, second inversion

i.　　　　　　　　ii.　　　　　　　iii.　　　　　　　iv.　　　　　　　v.

8. Write the following scales ascending and descending in whole notes using a key signature for each.

G flat major

F minor, melodic form

B flat minor, harmonic form

F sharp major

The enharmonic tonic major of C sharp major

9. For the following melody: Name the key. At the end of each phrase write the functional and root/quality chord symbols and name each cadence as half, perfect authentic, or imperfect authentic.

key: _____   Cadence: _____

Cadence: _____

10. Match each statement with the best answer.

a. Composer of Brandenburg Concerto No. 5
b. Classical Period
c. Also known as Serenade No. 13 for strings
d. Composer of Eine kleine Nachtmusik
e. One of the sections found in Sonata form
f. Compostion using 2 part counterpoint
g. Genre of this work is Concerto Grosso
h. Short melodic or rhythmic idea
i. Baroque period

_____ Motive
_____ Brandenburg Concerto No. 5
_____ Wolfgang Amadeus Mozart
_____ ca. 1600 -1750
_____ Invention in C, BWV 772
_____ Eine kleine Nachtmusik
_____ Development
_____ ca. 1750 -1825
_____ Johann Sebastian Bach

11. Define the following musical terms.

a. *animato*   _____
b. *con fuoco*   _____
c. *piu mosso*   _____
d. *senza*   _____
e. *subito*   _____

©San Marco Publications 2022

12. Analyze the following musical excerpt by answering the questions.

Ludwig van Beethoven
(1770- 1827)

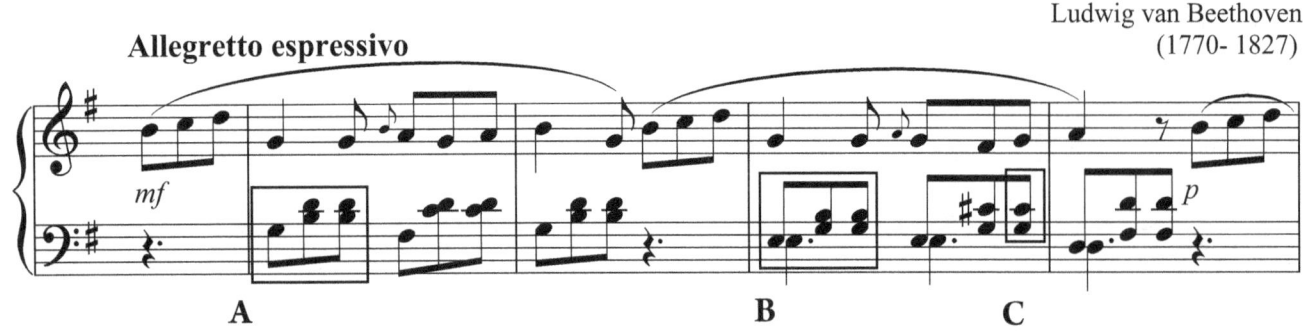

1. What is the key of this piece? _____

2. Write the time signature on the score.

3. In what era was this composed? _____

4. Define *Allegretto espressivo* _____

5. For the triad at A, name the: Root: _____ Quality: _____ Inversion: _____

6. For the triad at B, name the: Root: _____ Quality: _____ Inversion: _____

7. Find a diatonic half step in the score. Circle it and label it: DHS.

8. Find a broken C major triad on the score. Circle it and label it: C major.

9. Name the interval at C. _____

www.ingramcontent.com/pod-product-compliance
Lightning Source LLC
Chambersburg PA
CBHW081621100526
44590CB00021B/3537